Divinity Dice presents: Decimal Dice

DECIMAL DICE WORKBOOK

Your Manual for Divining with the 10 Sided Die

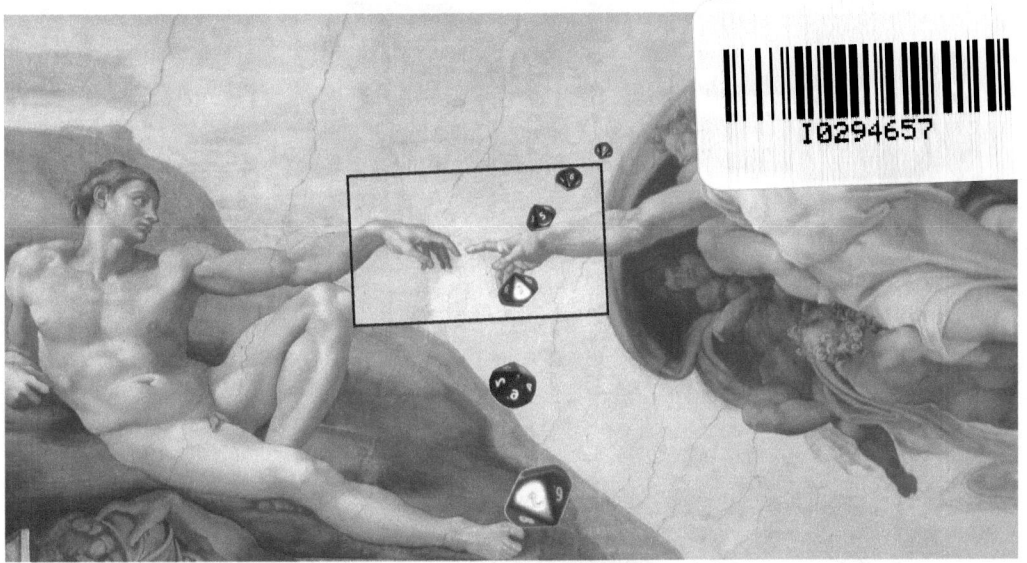

"Iacta alea est."
(Let the Dice Fly High)
Julius Caesar

Learn the Secrets of the 10 Sided Dice

Let the "Dice of the Gods" answer your most secret questions. As you play you will discover that underneath appearances Hidden Patterns are at work, which you can discover and work with to improve your life, make more money,

Author: Michael J Wallace

Containing Books One, Two and Three of the Decimal Dice Series

DISCLAIMER

The Decimal Dice Workbook is a technical publication that describes detailed ways in which we can resolve Number Patterns using Ten Sided Dice. At no time does either the publisher or author assert that this book will provide you with a way to foretell the future.

COPYRIGHT 2006-2015 Michael Wallace

This book is published under the Berne Convention. All copyright protected to the author. No prior use without permission except for excerpts for review or educational purposes. All enquiries via Email to: **info.numberharmonics@gmail.com**
 Published by Ladder to the Moon c/o PO Box 1355 Kingscliff NSW 2487.
 All rights reserved to the copyright holder.

Decimal Dice Workbook
Divining with the 10 Sided Die

Containing the Original Trilogy of Decimal Dice books:

- **Book One:** Let the Dice Fly High   Page 4
- **Book Two:** Pythagorean Trines   Page 19
- **Book Three:** Advanced Games   Page 97

Extracted from the Complete Divinity Dice Transcripts.
Compiled under the auspices of the Pythagorean Guild

Author: Michael J Wallace
Copyright 2006-2015 M. Wallace

"If you are into Divining with Dice, you owe it to yourself to take a good look at the Divinity Dice books."
Luke Rhinehart, "The Diceman" (AKA Prof George Cockroft)

Decimal Dice Workbook

BOOK ONE:
Let the Dice Fly High

This introductory section is a booklet of Games, and with all games, there are rules. The first rule is, there are hardly any rules!

All this entails is simply adding things up and making sense out of what answers come to you. This is a series of games where you follow a pattern, and it leads you to an answer. Let your INTUITION guide you. Of course: The more you practice, the better your intuition will become.

How it Works: Ask a question, throw the Dice according to the games we show you here, and you get these amazing and interesting interpretations. But it doesn't stop there... Getting an Interpretation is the start, now YOU have to figure out how this connects to the question.

When you put the Question alongside the Interpretation, you find lots of options start opening up, and many answers seem to come your way. So now you may need to re-qualify the question, and throw the Dice again! Try a different Game, and see what comes of it.

That's how it works. It can also be great fun to have a group of people all putting in their view. Dice Satsang it is called: Satsang simply means "Gathering".

The one detail you will have to understand is a thing called SIMPLE ARITHMETIC. You may throw the 10 Sided Dice three times and get the numbers: 9, 5, 8. Add these together, to get 22. THEN we can add the 22 DOWN to get 4. (2+2 = 4) This is, as it says, arithmetic that is simple. Just add down the numbers you add up.

The rest is simply following the "form" or technique we show you, finding the Interpretations, and working it out from there.

Have fun, enjoy the process, and show your friends. Practice on people you meet, and soon enough you will be the hit of the party. If you need help, go to **divinitydice.com.au** for info.

Dice Games are very old. This Roman Plate shows Venus playing Dice with Pan

From the FIRST unto the SECOND where

www.numberharmonics.org

Decimal Dice Workbook　　　　　　　　Six Box Technique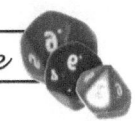

Let's Practice throwing the Dice: 6 Box Technique

We all want instant answers to our questions, and this is a great way to start. This is the 6 Box Technique. The way it works is simple. First: ASK A QUESTION. Let's invent a question. It could be anything: Does that Girl fancy me? Will I get that new job? Etc.

A Quick Focus on the Question: Maybe you are asking "How does this new promotion look?" Finding the right question is the hard part. You are not "really" wanting to know how a promotion LOOKS are you? You are wanting to know if it is a step in the right direction, if you will enjoy the new challenges, if it will be worthwhile, etc.

So STOP and focus on the question first. Qualify it. "Does this new promotion enhance my career?" is a better question, but what is "your career"? Get it? We are looking for the HEART of the Question you want to know. Underneath it all, what you need to know what your direction is in this present moment, and it happens to be a job that is staring you in the face that is the main concern.

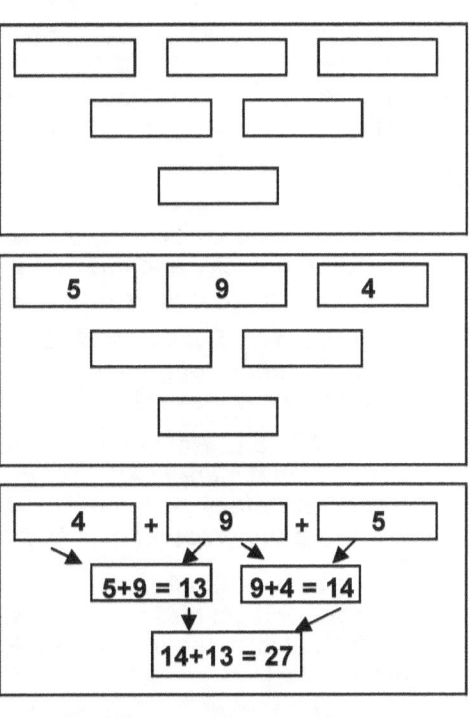

After the finding question, the rest is easy. Draw a series of boxes like those in the top graphic. The meaning for these is over the page.

Next we throw the 10 Sided Dice THREE times. Let's say you throw a 4, 9 and 5; write these numbers into the three boxes. (The second diagram) . So far, so good. Now we simply add the numbers together in the way we show you..

We add the 4 and 9 to get 13 and write it into the box under and between their "place" Likewise we add the 9 and the 5 to get 14 and place this addition in the box allocated. Now we add the 13 and the 14 together, to get the Final Addition of 27. We see all the additions in the above graphics. Could it be any simpler? Now comes the tricky part.

The THIRD must then Appear (Paracelsus)

Decimal Dice Workbook

6 Box Technique: Continued

Your additions equal the three aspects of Past, Future and Present. Now we have to place the answers we get in each area in the context of the question asked, which is "What is my life path?". Now when we look at things, it will make simple and immediate sense.

The 13 represents the PAST, the 14 represents the FUTURE and the 27 represents the PRESENT. You asked about a new job, now look up the interpretations.

PAST: **13... You may be greatly misunderstood. Even so, this is not at all unlucky and indicates a new energy arriving in your life.**

FUTURE: **14... Snakes and Ladders: A number of movement, travel and new associations.**

PRESENT: **27... Reward will come from the application of intellect, not physical force. Growing the Intelligence of the Heart will bring the greatest of rewards.**

1st Dice	2nd Dice	3rd Dice
PAST	FUTURE	
	PRESENT	

4	+	9	+	5
	4+9 = 13		9+5 = 14	
		14+13 = 27		

So, you asked about where you are at the moment. You threw the Dice and you got these interpretations. Can you make any sense out of it? The first response is often "Hell, this looks complicated!". But really, it isn't.

In the Past, concerning the direction you have taken, you have been misunderstood. Maybe you didn't understand yourself, or someone else has been the issue? Even so, it is not unlucky, and from the PAST a new energy is coming. So, the message is: Look for someone or something from your PAST. Get it?

The FUTURE says "Movement, Travel, New Associations" Does this new promotion offer this? If it doesn't, it does not fit into your future direction, so maybe you need to look further.

The PRESENT says to apply intellect, not force. You can't push things at the moment. Do you need more education? If you are in a physical job, it may be saying "get out of this field". It also speaks of growing the Intelligence of the Heart. (Huh? You ask, "What's that?")

From the FIRST unto the SECOND where

www.numberharmonics.org

Decimal Dice Workbook — *Six Box Technique*

6 Box Technique: Continued

What does "Grow the intelligence of the Heart" mean? Well, that is something for you to consider. It was considered the highest of all attributes in Ancient Egypt. IE: To be able to see clearly with the heart.

So far, your reading is saying that if the promotion involves travel, new people and movement, it is a good thing to go for. It is also saying that you will get to this "future" possibility through the use of Intelligence, not force. This could be saying it is a "Who you know" position that is coming up, and you better start working the connections if you want the job. Getting the idea of how it works?

You are given the pieces to the Jigsaw puzzle, but you have to find the way the pieces fit together best. And you may have to give it a few throws until you start to get the message.

All the interpretations for every number between 1 and 60 are at Page 36 of this booklet. Practice this simple Game, because it really works.

You can take this game one step further. Add up ALL the Past, Present and Future numbers to get an overall number. In this case 14 + 13 + 27 = 54. Look up 54 in the Composite Numbers, and we get: 54... Reaching the Stars requires letting go of the Earth. Get it? You have to let go of your fears, and just get on with it.

Now, sometimes the additions of Past, Future, and Present come to over the number 60. If you threw 9, 9 and 9 you would get additions of 18 + 18 + 36 = 72. Simple: Add the 72 to get (7+2 = 9) NINE.

That's it! That is all there is to the Six Box Game. You can play this at parties, and all you need is this little book, your 10 sided dice, and some interested people. The real trick, as we mentioned, is to get the RIGHT QUESTION. Asking the Right question is like opening the right door. Some basic considerations for you may be:
- Career: What is it that you "really" want? Are you looking for purpose, money, prestige, security or just to get by because you have other interests?
- Love: Are you looking for Love, or Sex? Are you wanting a long term faithful relationship, or something exciting?
- Finance: Are you prepared to go out on a limb? Are you willing to risk everything on a toss of the coin? What are your limits?

Play this game, and get to know the "real" you a whole lot more!

The THIRD must then Appear (Paracelsus)

Decimal Dice Workbook

6 Box Technique: Continued

OK... Final Page of the Six Box technique. The process so far is:
1. We throw the 10 sided dice three times
2. We write down the numbers, and add them up
3. We look up the interpretations, and finally
4. We try to make some sense out of it all.

The key to getting good answers is asking the right questions. Often we have to throw the Dice several times, and the Dice themselves often offer interpretations that will lead you to ask better questions.

It's all a "go with the Flow" thing. Trust your instincts, and work out what it really is that you want to know. *A perfect example came from a tarot card reader I knew.* A fellow came in to the reader asking if he was going to become a world famous writer. The reader saw it was really a fellow who just wanted to escape the public service, so he urged him to qualify his question.

"Why not ask if you are going to become famous, or more to the point ask if you are going to become a GOOD writer. I know for a fact there are only a handful of famous writers on the planet, so maybe we need to focus on what do you REALLY want to know?

The fellow said, flatly, that he wanted to know if he was to become a famous writer. Nothing else would do. So the tarot card reader laid out the cards, and told him he would marry a nice girl, have three children and be quite happy in this life.

I asked him later, "What did the cards REALLY say to his question. "Oh," he answered, "they clearly suggested he may well be a famous writer. "Well ... Why didn't you tell him?" I asked. His answer always stayed with me to this very day. "Now now, if I told him he was really going to be a famous writer, he may go do something really foolish and leave his job. If he is going to be what he is going to be, it surely doesn't need a mere tarot card reader like me to set him straight!"

That's the real truth. No matter what comes up, the future is really in YOUR hands. The dice may offer you clues as to the Frame of your Destiny, but YOU are the one who chooses what picture to hang in it.

Relax, have fun, and don't take it too seriously. You will be amazed at the uncanny accuracy of the readings, but take it easy because your journey of Dice Divination has just begun.

From the FIRST unto the SECOND where

Decimal Dice Workbook — Finding Doublets

Finding Doublets in the Matrix: 9 Box Technique

Below we see the traditional Number Positions for the Pythagorean Matrix. It is quite simple; the lower left box is the starting point, and the upper Right Box is the end. You write down your throw of the dice according the order in which it is thrown

Each throw of the Dice places a number "over" the top of the pre-existing position. Below we show you the basic idea. Again, we are using the 10 Sided Dice. We throw this Dice TEN TIMES, and place the numbers thrown in the traditional order, as shown in "Nine Boxes" to your left. The graphic is self explanatory. You throw the numbers (in this order): 3, 7, 9, 0, 1, 2, 6, 1 and 1

Order of Your Throws

3	6	9
2	5	8
1	4	7

+

The Numbers Thrown

9	2	1
7	1	1
3	0	6

=

Now we COMBINE the throw with the pre-ordained Number Position. It gives us a combination of Double Numbers that combines the ORDER of the throw, with the throw itself

3/9 6/2 9/1
2/7 5/1 8/1
1/3 4/0 7/6

NOTE: the FORTH casting of the Dice gives 4/0. Consider this a "blank" for now. We will not go into the significance of this here.

We now have a PATTERN OF NUMBER to work with. Always try to remember, when we are working with the Dice, we are looking for a Pattern of Number that relates to one or more of the interpretations.

The Next stage is to simple look up the meanings of these, and with your question in mind, see what picture forms out of it. (over)

The THIRD must then Appear (Paracelsus)

www.numberharmonics.org

9 Box Technique: Continued

Interpretations are on Page 114. For this cast they are:

1/3 Big plans, but often insecure
2/7 Balance the Masculine and Feminine within
3/9 Take care with appearing pretentious
4/0 (Zero Dice casting. Has significance, but too detailed for here)
5/1 Ego whispers the most cunning truth
6/2 Can you see yourself in the mirror
7/6 Get over the hump and the new day awaits
8/1 Throw caution to the wind carefully
9/1 Knowing what to say is half the battle

It is amazing how clearly a message is formed. Just by reading through the interpretations, the concepts in regards an answer to your question starts to form.

Imagine if your question was about Travel to India this year. You can see easily how a message will form through the INTERACTION of the interpretation with the question. See what the Dice say to you with the Travel question then, for practice, change the question.

Now imagine you are asking about your current relationship. Can you see how the above "interpretation" will adjust and give new insights into this area as well? A whole set of different aspects will highlight themselves. This is what makes this technique so good at parties.

Can you see that with this combination of throws there are three ONE's in the position of the 5, 8 and 9? This forms a TRINE which also has a meaning. (We take this up later in Advanced Games)

In summary, getting clear results from ALL Divinity Dice techniques comes down to the Question you ask. More specifically, it all hinges on the sort of questions you are asking. Try it... Ask a question, throw the dice, and see what comes of it. Remember: ASK YOUR QUESTION FIRST. Preferably, take a sheet of paper, and write the question down on the sheet of paper you will work with.

Work out your Matrix Map, throw the 10 sided dice Nine Times and write down the numbers in order of their appearance in the boxes as we have discussed. That's it for the Double Number Technique.

Just this process on its own is enough to solve many concerns.

9 Box Technique: Continued

Let's look at this again. We have the basic Graphic as shown to the right.

3	6	9
2	5	8
1	4	7

We throw the Dice NINE TIMES in order to find a number to match against the "original" number. This gives us the Double Number, or Doublet.

We look up the Double Number and see what the flow of interpretations adds up when we compare it against the question we have in mind. Could it be any simpler?

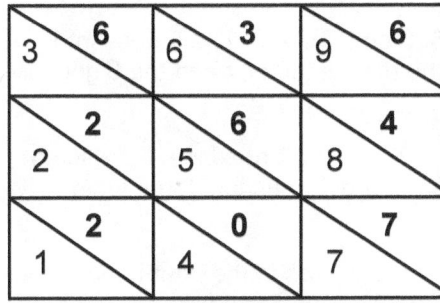

Let's look at another example. First, and as always, we ASK A QUESTION. We throw the 10 Sided Dice nine times, and we come up with the following Numbers: 2, 2, 6, 0, 6, 3, 7, 4 and 6. We write these into the Pattern to our Right against the "original" number positions to get the graph as shown.

This gives us the Double Numbers of: 1/2, 2/2, 3/6, 4./0, 5/6, 6/3, 7/7, 8/4 and 9/6 which we now look up in the Double Number Interpretations on pages 22 to 23. These are as follows:

    1/2 **Creative, often indecisive you ask what to do**
    2/2 **Time to Decide**
    3/6 **Mind your Mind, Care for the Heart**
    4/0 **No specific Meaning**
    5/6 **Your Path is clear now, Decide**
    6/3 **Thinking is good when it serves a purpose**
    7/7 **Risk is called for. Look to Act**
    8/4 **Power must be matched with compassion**
    9/6 **Careful consideration is called for**

Obviously, the Die is saying it is time to decide, and that there is a risk. However, consideration of the heart of things, both for self and for others, will pay dividends. Not so hard, is it?

The THIRD must then Appear (Paracelsus)

Decimal Dice Workbook

The Matrix Map Reading Game

This is a form of Divination (using the 10 sided Dice) that closely follows the principles of the Pythagorean School.

We expand on the 9 Square Technique of the previous pages, and move into the Pythagorean Matrix Map. This follows the archetypal patterns we call the "Lines of Force". This is all done according to the traditional polarities, but if you think about it, the Eight Archetypes are universal and transcend the ages. As always, ASK YOUR QUESTION before you throw the dice.

The ORDER in which you write down your throws of the Dice is important. Starting from the bottom left corner and running up to the top left corner, throw your TEN SIDED DICE (three times per row). Write down the number value (as shown) in the appropriate box.

LEFT Column: Let's say you threw 5, then 7, then 9. The 5 goes into the bottom left box, the 7 goes into the middle left box and the 9 goes into the top left box.

MIDDLE Column: Next you throw 2, 4 and 0 ... 2 goes into the middle bottom box, 4 goes into the central box, and 0 goes into the middle top box.

RIGHT Column: Do this for the next three throws in the right hand boxes... say it is 3, 9 and 1. 3 goes into the right bottom box. 9 goes into the right middle box and 1 goes into the right top box.

This means we now have a map that looks like what you see on the opposite page. Now we add the various rows and diagonals, and write the additions into the Box provided. Add all the horizontal, vertical and diagonal rows, and place them in the appropriate box

We now add the first addition of the "lines" to get to a single number. This is the process called "Simple Addition" (Refer Page 2) On the following page we give the Matrix Map with the throws of the dice filled in, including the additions on the sheet (As you will normally do them) and the additions in a graph (As you would normally do them)

These rows are added as follows: (Graphic opposite) On the page 10 we give an interpretation for this casting of the dice.

Decimal Dice Workbook  *Matrix Map*

MATRIX MAP EXAMPLE

	BUSINESS / CREATIVE	AMBITION / GOALS	ALTRUISM / IDEALS	
SERVICE / COMPASSION	21/3	6	13/4	10/1
MENTAL	9	0	1	10/1
EMOTIONAL	7	4	9	20/2
PHYSICAL	5	2	3	10/1
SUCCESS / DESIRE				16/7

Business / Creative:	5+7+9 = 21 2+1 = **3**	**Physical:**	5+2+3 = 10 1+0 = **1**
Ambition / Goals:	2+4+0 = **6**	**Emotional:**	7+4+9 = 20 2+0 = **2**
Altruism / ideals	3+9+1 = 13 1+3 = **4**	**Mental:**	9+0+1 = 10 1+0 = **1**
Success / Desire:	5+4+1 = 10 1+0 = **1**	**Service / Compassion:**	9+4+3 = 16 1+6 = **7**

The THIRD must then Appear (Paracelsus)

www.numberharmonics.org

Decimal Dice Workbook

How to Interpret the Matrix Map

Let's say your question is "What is the best way for me to resolve the sense of frustration I feel with this (whatever) relationship?" Remember the question can change, and indeed, expect it to change if you are doing it right. Now we look at the additions, placing the meaning over the Line affected, and over the question we have in mind. The archetypal meaning for each "line" is Ancient, but the dice, combined with the question, will put a new life into it for you.

Look up the additions in the Composite Number Interpretations, and see what you make of it. (Actual Interpretations start on Page 36)

The Physical says "ONE" ... This can mean look at yourself, look at how you have your one-ness in order. But look up the general meaning, and keep it in mind as you move onto the next line.

The Emotional says "TWO" which can indicate that in your emotions you are running on two streams of feeling. It can mean you are trapped in the fight or flight response.

The Mental says "ONE". Are you too solitary and too single minded?

Your Business/Creative says "THREE". This indicates you need to plan things and allow your creative energy to flow more. Maybe you need to take up poetry?

The Ambition / Goals say "**SIX**". This is the number of Family, Business and Intuition, so it is saying look at this area in particular.

The Altruism / Ideals say "FOUR" which tends to indicate a need for stability. Have you been too generous with your time helping others and not getting a real return from this? Maybe you need to take stock with the human reality of your ideals?

Your Success / Desire states "ONE". Another One... You have Three Ones, which means the ONE is the significant energy and the One is associated with Vitality and being physically active, so maybe the issue of your frustration is simply that you are not being active enough... You are not getting your physical energy moving, and you are blocking yourself because of this.

Your Service / Compassion states "SEVEN" ... So in the area of where you connect with others, the Seven is there. Are you being too secretive? Are you being too insular? Do you need to be more social?

Decimal Dice Workbook *Matrix Map*

Interpretation: Now what we do is to add ALL the numbers throw to get an Overview or Ruling Number. 5, 7, 9, 2, 4, 0, 3, 9 and 1 all add to 40. Look up Forty in the Composite Numbers to get the overview of the reading: Which indicates ... ***self containment, and possible isolation as needed, to work out the inner questions.***

Now, to the question in regards a relationship. Your Physical, Emotional and Mental Lines are all looking at YOU. This means that you are working out something inside yourself, which means to not look at a solution from the other person in your question.

Your Ideals, Goals and Business are talking about organizing and spending time with family. Family is important, look closely at this area. There is more here than meets the eye

And the Success is a ONE, more about YOU, with the Compassion and Service Line speaking of SEVEN. Seven is like a bridge between your outer and your inner world, and so the reading is really saying the problem is with you communicating your inner self. The concern is not the outer relationship, but your INNER relationship with yourself.

From the nature of the question, there is obviously some difficulty on the horizon. How do you solve it? The dice are saying that you will need to be more physically active (All the Ones), and to get out there and be less "internal" (The Seven). Maybe you just need to find a hobby or interest that takes up your energy and your attention, and gives you an avenue of communication. Get the idea? Allow the story to grow from the numbers, and you will be amazed how easily it builds to a solution to the question you have.

In all, you have NINE throws of the Ten Sided Dice. Using the numbers from these throws you place them into the Matrix Map, then add up all the "lines" in this map... Eight in all. Place the simple addition of the three numbers from each line into the box provided, and look up the meaning of that number... Then INTERPRET what you see. As you practice this simple technique you will get the idea. The answers you get will often astound you with their uncanny accuracy.

ADDITIONAL STUDIES:

There are deeper aspects to the Matrix Map, regarding Trines and Double Numbers (Doublets). We touch on the Doublets in the last exercise. Trines are found in Book Two (*Pythagorean Trines*) and a larger view of the Matrix is in Book Three, *Advanced Games*.

Decimal Dice Workbook

Go Get to that Party and get some Practice !!

The ideas in this section are all great party games. They are light and fun. It is recommended that you practice with the Dice on your friends and family but when you get your confidence up, give it a go at parties! It is all light and easy, and a great ice breaker. What is more, a 10 sided Dice, a pen and this booklet is all you will need to really impress people. You too can be the centre of attention!

However, there is a serious side as well. As you get used to using the 10 Sided Dice, you may get interested in the more complex Decimal Dice Workbook, which gives deeper insight into some of these existing games, and goes into new techniques and games you can play.

Whatever you choose, people love the Dice games, and they love the thrill of having their "future" told. When people start asking questions about 'stuff' you will be amazed at how a group of people around you will hear what you have to say then come up with the most extraordinary insights for each question that comes up.

People have been using Dice for fun and divination for thousands of years, and as you find your feet, you will quickly start surprising yourself at how answers that really work and make sense will come to you with this simple game.

You can have great fun, and also possibly help others. Obviously, if you want to take it further and make some money doing readings, this doorway is open. It is up to you how far you want to take the Dice.

It's quicker to learn than a guitar, and can impress twice as much!

The Ancient Romans loved Dice.

They loved them so much, and they gambled so heavily, that at Times dicing was banned except for Saturnalia and other special festivals.

    The Romans believed that luck and opportunity were a way the Gods would speak to you.

    Dice games and gambling were thus tied in with a religious sense, and we find that even today a gambler will bless his "Lucky" dice.

A WALL DRAWING FROM POMPEII

From the FIRST unto the SECOND where

Decimal Dice Workbook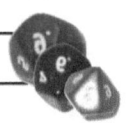

Now For the Interpretations! (Go To: Page 36)

Next we look at the Interpretations for what we have worked out so far. Here we use the FADIC Numbers, which start on Page 36. Please keep in mind that due to space restrictions, the indicated meanings for the Numbers 1 to 60 have been kept to an absolute minimum. Go to the Book of Aspects for more extended interpretations. This book is extensive and covers all aspects (except Patterns) found in Divinity Dice.

In all there are 81 Doublets, 60 Composites, 84 Trines, and 64 Patterns that form the basis for Interpretation within the Divinity Dice System.

If you wish to go to the pages of **www.numberharmonics.org** you will see a fascinating variation where we look at dates as random "throws" of number (Gods Dice?) and connect this to the Musical Scale. As a result, we have recreated the Ancient Tone Healing used by the Pythagoreans.

If you wish to learn more of the technical issues and information that are behind the Divinity Dice books, go to **divinitydice.com.au**

As you practice Dicing, you will be amazed at how one interpretation connects to the next, then to the next. It builds up an overview very quickly. Here we find two thing: Firstly, your initial question will start to change and modify as you get into the process of asking the Dice for answers. Almost every time, the "real" question we want answered is hiding behind the first questions we ask. That's a bit like life, you place one piece of the puzzle, and then the next one turns up to be placed.

Interpretations are like jigsaw pieces and we are looking to make a whole picture. One piece of the jigsaw will blend with the next one, and soon the full picture starts to emerge. Then it goes "click" and you get the message! It is a case where the sum of the parts is greater than the pieces.

When you get more familiar with the process, take a Dice book to a party, and watch the fun start! People are amazed at how accurate the results are, and the uncanny way the answers create a "bounce" of responses from everyone else is pretty amazing.

What we make very clear is that the Divinity Dice program is NOT fortune telling. It is meant to inspire and delight, and it is designed for you to have FUN. However, if you wish to take it further, and make this a professional money making business, we ask that you go through the tests and get accredited with the Pythagorean Guild. Go to **www.divinitydice.com.au** for more information

The THIRD must then Appear (Paracelsus)

Curious Dice Facts

In 1944, a Chicago resident, Louis Cohn, confessed that it was not Mrs. O'Leary's milk cow that started the Great Chicago Fire of 1891, but that he had excitedly knocked over a lantern during a winning streak while shooting craps.

Beautifully crafted dice games were among the treasures recovered from the tomb of Egypt's King Tutankhamen. (circa 1347-1339 BC)

It is claimed that dice were used during the Trojan War to keep spirits up between battles and missions.

During Christ's crucifixion, it has been noted that Roman soldiers tossed dice for his garments while standing guard.

When Caesar made the critical decision to take his victorious army across the Rubicon against the edict of Rome, he exclaimed: "lacta alea est." Some interpret this as "The die is cast" but modern scholars. looking at the psychology of Caesar suggest the better interpretation is "Let the Dice fly high" In other words, HE was the one trusting to his luck and throwing the dice, not merely dealing with the predestined chances the fates had already thrown.

The Emperor Commodus was fond of gambling with dice, and once turned the Imperial Palace into a brothel and gambling house to raise money for the treasury he bankrupted.

Gambling (in particular Dice Games incorporating gambling) became such an obsession for some Romans, and such a social problem in general, that the government was forced to restrict it. This was indeed unusual for the Romans, as they rarely restricted any type of civil or business activity. The Republic restricted gambling to the week-long festivities surrounding the Saturnalia (the modern Christmas & New Year's holidays).

Dice probably evolved from knucklebones, which are approximately tetrahedral Even today, dice are sometimes colloquially referred to as "bones". Ivory, bone, wood, metal, and stone materials have been commonly used, though the use of plastics is now nearly universal. It is almost impossible to trace clearly the development of dice from knucklebones, on account of the confusing of the two games by the ancient writers. It is certain, however, that both were played in times prior to which we possess any written records.

Decimal Dice Workbook

BOOK TWO: The Pythagorean Trines

Pythagorean TRINES

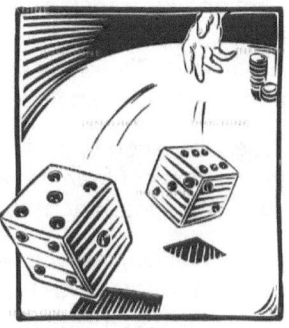

This book represents the first major reference to the 84 Sacred Trines of the old Pythagorean school in over 200 years.

The last known example of this aspect of the Pythagorean Teachings appeared in an 18th Century manuscript.

"Iacta alea est."
(Let the Dice Fly High)
Julius Caesar

INDEX:

Introduction .... Page 20
Instant Divination .... Page 22
Asking Questions .... Page 25
Finding the Trine .... Page 26
Find the Composite .... Page 28
Variations .... Page 30

Interpretations:

Composite Interpretations .... Page 36
Trine History and Info .... Page 46
Index for Trines .... Page 50
Rules for Understanding Trines .... Page 95

NOTICE: All interpretations and information in this book are under the Berne Convention. Divinity Dice and the author M Wallace authorizes the use of these and all interpretations in this book for personal use ONLY. Professional, promotional or any other use will be viewed as a breach of copyright. You can sit tests and be approved, however. We ask that you Email to **info.numberharmonics@gmail.com** for our requirements regarding professional use of the interpretations or forms as provided in this book.

The THIRD must then Appear (Paracelsus)

www.numberharmonics.org

Decimal Dice Workbook

INTRODUCTION: *What is Divination?*

First and foremost: The Art of True Divination is NOT going to some Fortune Teller and having them say what is going to happen to you. The Art of True Divination is NOT some witch doctor shaking feathers over animal entrails, and chanting mystical sounding words.

True Divination is an Art that requires a deep understanding of Self, and the process of learning to divine truth from outer symbols is really the start of the journey of divining truth from within yourself.

There is a Universal Law: *No person or thing can give you anything you do not already have.* It seems strange, because the Gifts of the Gods are many, but the saying means that unless we already have a seed of an idea within us already, all truth given is like water flowing over the top of a shallow glass.

A good example is the Oracle of Delphi, who when asked by a visiting King if a certain campaign would be successful, gave the enigmatic answer "When the river is crossed, a great King will fall."

The King leapt on this and presumed that he would defeat his opponent when he crossed the river separating their countries, but the Great King that fell was himself. He lost! The Oracle spoke the truth, but it is the person reading or hearing it who must grasp what it means?

The good news is, you are not expected to be perfect. These Games from Divinity Dice are designed as a Spiritual Growth Hormone, and the more you practice them with an open mind and heart, the more you will grow in understanding.

If you are going to get the most out of these books on Divining with Dice, what we suggest is that you just PLAY with it. Try not to force an understanding of what you read in the Interpretations. Let it "occur" to yourself as to what the meaning might be. An example: *Truth comes softly to the top of the glass you sip.* What does this somewhat cryptic message mean to you? In deciding the meaning, you are the diviner.

> **Pythagorean Trines come from the Ancient Pythagorean School** .
> This is an arcane tool of Divination. Here we give you techniques that associate specific "Oracles" to the random casting of Numbered Dice. In this Book we use the 10 Sided (Decimal) Die in various "Games" that lead us to specific answers to questions.

From the FIRST unto the SECOND where

www.numberharmonics.org

Decimal Dice Workbook

Playing the DECIMAL DICE Games:

*T*his Second book offers you a version of Divinity Dice that comes to us via an Oracular Dream by Robyn Keating. Here we use the 10 Sided Dice. Pythagoras introduced the Western World the Decimal system, and so it is appropriate to introduce you to the remarkable teachings of this individual via the Decimal Dice. NOTE: Always go to divinitydice.com.au for the latest updates

The Ten Sided Die is not one of the Platonic Solids (Sacred Solids of the Pythagoreans) yet they have a special place in the lexicon of Pythagorean Thought. Pythagoras discovered and practised the use of the Decimal System. It is considered likely that he either travelled to India, or at least studied under Vedic Mathematicians in Babylon. (He was taken there in 580BC) The Vedic System of Math had used the Base Ten (Decimal System) for thousands of years and many of the Pythagorean teachings can be seen to emanate from the "Sutras" or "Number Songs" of the fabled Indian mathematicians. (Including the now famous 3-4-5 triangle proof we call the Pythagorean Theorem)

Prior to Pythagoras, Western Math was based on the Base 12 and Base 60 systems (even though the Decimal System was in limited use). These "archaic" maths had distinct advantages in calculating building principles, but both systems were hard to grasp and so the Science of Mathematics remained in the hands of a chosen elite few.

The Pythagoreans broke this cloistered environment. By putting Math (amongst other things) into common language the Pythagorean Universities created education for all. The Pythagorean Universities were considered the Harvard's, Yale's and Oxford's of their day, and were highly respected. *It is worth noting that the Pythagoreans broke with tradition and permitted women to the hallowed halls of learning.*

In Pythagorean Trines (a book in the Decimal Dice series) we employ simple yet extremely deep methods to gain an answer to a question or situation that may be troubling you. There are several ways to work out an interpretation and several ways to throw the 10 sided dice.

As you go through the following pages, look at every section and make sure you grasp it before moving onto the next. If you do this, the whole thing will become very easy to grasp, and you will be astounding your friends in no time at all.

Decimal Dice Workbook

So... What's involved with all of this?

Throw the Die in a set Game and add the numbers shown to either a Number Combination. between One and Sixty, or you will get a set of Three Numbers, which form a Pythagorean Trine.

In a nutshell, that's about it. We cast the 10 Sided Dice in various Games to get Number Patterns which lead us to certain interpretations.

We are adding things up, and adding things down, and looking for hidden patterns, but all in all it you will come to either a number between One and Sixty, which is called a Composite Number, or a set of three different Numbers between One and Nine, called a Trine.

Most of this book involves written meanings for the above aspects. The first thing we need to learn are a few little "games" that show you how to play with all of this. Let's start with some of the most basic game, below, to get you into the swing of things.

Instant Divination Game:
One Throw, One Number, One Meaning

The most basic of all Dice Games is just to throw the dice, and see what number rolls up for you. The way we do this is as follows:

- **First and Foremost and ALWAYS: Ask a Question!**
- **Second: Throw the Die, and see what number turns up**
- **Third: Find that Number in the Composite Number Interpretations, at Page 35, and look up what it means.**

EG: If you throw an Eight, you read the Eight Interpretation. Now we have to apply this interpretation to the question you have asked.

Let's say you asked about dating some person. The 8 says: "Reap the Harvest. What is in this moment that you can gather? Inspect the fruit, then prune the tree accordingly." Now you just have to sort out what this means to you! (And it doesn't always mean something right away)

The Die MAY be saying to check out the person's parents and family before committing yourself. They may be putting on one face to you, but another to them. It may be that this person is a gift from the Gods, and someone you have worked hard to meet. So enjoy the fruit! Get it?

From the FIRST unto the SECOND where

Decimal Dice Workbook

Welcome to the Pythagorean Trines

This is a book of Divination Games, and with all games, there are rules. Our first rule is, there are hardly any rules!

Everything here is simply mathematics of some sort. We are adding up in various ways the throw of the Die, and then making sense out of the answer that comes. In all we are looking for a Number Pattern which leads us to an interpretation. Simple. Trust your INTUITION and the answers will just go "Click". The more you practice, the better you get.

How it Works is simple: Ask a question, throw the Dice according to the games shown here, and you discover amazing and interesting interpretations. But it doesn't stop here… Getting an Interpretation is just the start. Now YOU have to figure out how this connects to your question.

When you put the Question alongside the Interpretation, you find lots of options start opening up, and many answers seem to come your way. So now you may need to re-qualify the question, and throw the Dice again! Try a different Game, and see what comes of it.

The Trines themselves derive from all the possible combinations of the Numbers One to Nine which never repeat themselves. There are 84 in all, and the curious connection to the Vedic Principle called the "Wheel of 84" or the Wheel of Karma cannot be avoided.

These specific Trines are ARCHETYPAL PATTERNS that have great portent and meaning. They hold powerful and clear messages for you.

Just follow techniques we show you and it will be made clear enough how it works. This book is only using what we call the COMPOSITE Numbers, and TRINES. Both are cut down interpretations from The Book of Aspects. We also include in this book Advanced Dice Games as the Third Section. And if you want to go further, you can! Because there's MORE

Have fun, enjoy the process, and show your friends. Practice on people you meet, and soon enough you will be the hit of the party.

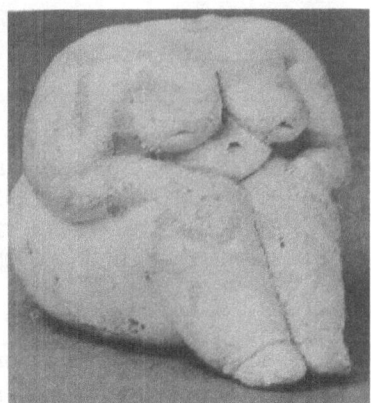

Cybelle: Primary Roman Goddess

The THIRD must then Appear (Paracelsus)

www.numberharmonics.org

Decimal Dice Workbook

The Step By Step of Die Casting

There is very little to understand about casting the Die... You just throw it and see what turns up. Obviously, a 10 Sided Die will only give a number between Zero and Nine, as pictured to the Right.

You will either be adding up the Dice thrown, or seeing if there is a combination of Three different numbers that comes about, which is called a TRINE. We are looking to create a Number Pattern. Let's look at examples:

Example ONE: You throw the numbers: 9, 2 and 7

This creates three different Number and, rearranged from Lowest to Highest, we have a 2-7-9 TRINE.

Example TWO: You throw the Numbers 1, 4, 4

This does NOT form a Trine, but we can ADD the numbers to get **1+4+4 = 9**. Look up the Interpretation for the Number 9.

Example THREE: You throw the Numbers 0, 8, 7

Zero does not have a value, so it is not 3 different numbers to form a Trine. Add **8 + 7 = 15** and look up the interpretation for 15 **OR** you can add 15 to **1+5 = 6** and look up the 6.

Example FOUR: You throw Numbers 1, 5, 7, 3, 9

It looks as if there are LOTS of Trines here, but as a rule, when looking for a Trine you stop at the first three numbers that are different in a single throw. In this case, 1-5-7. But ALSO add them up and see what comes! **1+5+7+3+9 = 23** so we can look up 23 OR we can add it down to **2+3 = 5** and look up the 5.

Get the idea? We are looking for a TRINE of 3 different numbers or a COMPOSITE, which is a Number between 1 and 60. No matter what way you throw the Die you will end up with either of these.

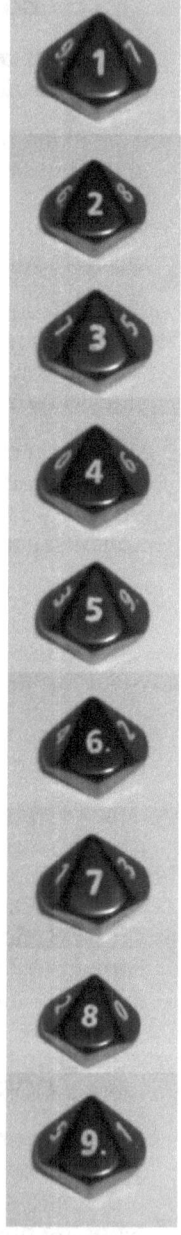

From the FIRST unto the SECOND where

www.numberharmonics.org

ASKING THE QUESTION

The core of making sense out of any of the Games and techniques we show you here is asking the right Question to begin with. Ask the right question, and the interpretations make a lot more sense. The Right Answers comes from the Right Question, in other words.

An old Tibetan Saying: **In all questions the answer is a seed.** *This means that* if you can frame the question, you can find the answer. So let's look at the Art of Question asking.

FIRST: *Curiosity or Need?* We must define the importance in every question we ask. Is it a simple curiosity or an absolute need? There is a point between these where our Question sits.

Let's look at a simple question like "What's the weather going to be tomorrow?" WHY are we asking this? It is important and NEED BASED if you are going to harvest wheat or go on a holiday. But If you are going for a walk, it is simply a question of curiosity. You may NEED to take a raincoat, however. The first step in asking a question is defining for yourself the level of importance or NEED in the answer.

SECOND: *Vague or Specific?* Questions can be SPECIFIC or VAGUE. We must refine the Question to ask SPECIFICALLY what we want to know, and to do this we need to know what we want.

Don't be concerned if you can't resolve your question right away. It is a skill that takes time to develop. In fact, you can use the Dice to assist you to refine what you want to know. Ask a question, throw the Die, look up the answer, and let it lead you to another question.

Getting specific is one of the more difficult things to master. As an example, you may wish to know about a future partner. Should you marry this person? This sort of question has THOUSANDS of side issues that run off it. Is there a better partner on the way? Will it last?, etc. etc. However if you focus the question on what you NEED you can get a clearer answer.

Ask about what you NEED. *Will this person remain faithful? Will this person stay kind? Are there hidden secrets here?* These are questions that will get you clearer answers regarding a life partner.

The THIRD must then Appear (Paracelsus)

Decimal Dice Workbook

Finding the Trine:

This are many ways to get an answer from the dice. Finding the Trine is a basic technique, however. If you really focus on these next pages, soon you will be a Divinity Dice Pro.

FIRST: As always! Ask a question or pose a thought based on something that you want an answer to.

SECOND: Take the TEN SIDED die and throw it. Write down the numbers cast on a sheet of paper. (I recommend using a graph like we show you below) *Keep doing this until you get a run of three different numbers.* STOP when you get a run of **three different numbers**.

Let's say you throw, 7, 6, 6, 4, 8 ... Stop here, because you have a **series of three different numbers**: 6, 4 and 8. These numbers form the 4.6.8 TRINE. *Look this up in the Trine Interpretations, and you will have the first part to an "Instant Answer" to your question.*

Next add ALL the number values you have thrown to date. In this case add the following: 7+6+6+4+8 = 31. 31 is the COMPOSITE Number of this throw. But please note how in the graphic I add the numbers in steps. (7+6=13 / 13+6=19 / 19+4=23 / 23+8=31) More on this on page 12. Look up the definition for 31 in the Composite interpretations and also the meaning for the 4.6.8 Trine. Is there a connection?

This is the First Game of *Pythagorean Trines* to master. First we have to get to know the Trines a little better, and to start to grasp the significance and meaning behind the various number combinations of Trine and Composite. I provide here a graphic that you can use to make it easier to follow the pattern of what to do with this section:

Layout for a throw of Numbers using 10 sided dice:

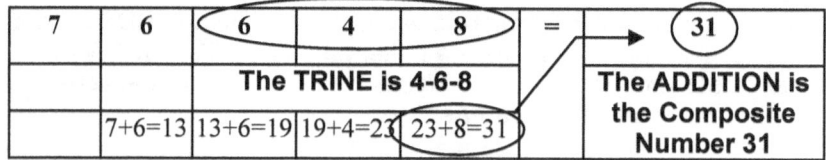

Your Answer is found with the Interpretation for the 4-6-8 TRINE and the 31 COMPOSITE. Imagine your question is about career. How does the following add up?

Decimal Dice Workbook — *Find the Trine*

- *4-6-8 Trine: Freedom is found in the Little Things. Keep a record of your thoughts. Self Sufficiency is Important.*
- *31 Composite: Your ability to communicate with others is what will open the door for you.*

As you can see, it is a self-evident answer regarding Career, but it may be about Love. How would this alter the way you look at the above?

Now it is your turn....

THROW #	1st	2nd	3rd	4th	5th	6th	7th	8th	9th	10th
NUMBER										
ADDITION										

Try throwing your own dice. Throw the TEN SIDED DICE and write down each number in the box, running from left to right. Stop as soon as you get your first THREE SEPARATE NUMBERS. This is your TRINE. This Trine relates to your question in some way. *Remember to arrange the numbers in your Trine from Lowest to Highest, which will make is much easier to find in the Interpretations starting on Page 100.*

Next: ADD all the numbers you have just throw together so you can reach your First Addition. This is called the COMPOSITE. Add up all the numbers like we did in the first exercise, and now you have the option of looking up the "string" of Number. In the first exercise this was 7, 13, 19, 23 and 31 ... Look it up, and see what you see

Give this idea a couple of tries. Throw the Dice until you find the Trine, then add up all the numbers thrown to find the Composite.

Use an open grid like the sample below when calculating the pattern of numbers. Remember to STOP when you have three different numbers. The FIRST THREE NUMBERS that are DIFFERENT form a TRINE and this is when you stop and do the additions.

Also remember that this is really a game of between One and Nine. If your dice has a Zero or a Ten on its face this is counted as Zero in this game. It is up to you whether the Zero throw counts as a "Start again" or as part of the Number series. You may even consider this as an indicator there is the element of Spirit (void) working in this reading. YOU decide what YOUR answer is. You are now the Oracle

Simple... that's it! First level completed.

The THIRD must then Appear (Paracelsus)

www.numberharmonics.org

Decimal Dice Workbook

Finding the COMPOSITE NUMBERS :

We can take the simple idea from the previous pages, but now generate a greater field of numbers to consider. If we wish to extend our example of the previous page, here is an easy way to do it.

ADDITIONS

	7+6 = 13	13+6 = 19	19+4 = 23	23+8 = 31		
7	6	6	4	8	=	31
		\multicolumn{3}{c}{4-6-8 TRINE}		COMPOSITE

Please note: Always put the Numbers in any Trine in an order from the lowest to Highest. This makes it much easy to look up when you want to find the interpretation. (Page 30 has the Index)

As you can see, we are simply adding each number together from Left to Right, and getting a number value as we do so. It is very simple… If you can add, you can work it out. Here we see a new series of number that we can read the Composite Values for, and see if there is a pattern we can see in the "thread" of Number. (There always is, by the way, it is just up to us to find it)

The Additions are: 7 / 7+6 = 13 / 13+6 = 19 / 19+4 = 23 / 23+8 = 31

Now we look up the Numbers below (at Pages 21 to 29) for the COMPOSITE INTERPRETATIONS: 7 / 13 / 19 / 23 / 31

As we look through the interpretations for this series of number, does a picture start to form? Does any image or idea come to you that seem to link all these numbers together in a single thread? Once more, there always is a connecting thread, we just have to see it.

Try practicing with a few throws of your own. We are initially looking for a TRINE, but we are also looking for the COMPOSITE NUMBERS to create a greater "Field of Number" to harvest.

Remember: *Stop when you get the first set of three different numbers!* Add up the numbers in the order they are thrown, and rearrange the last set of 3 different numbers from lowest to highest to form a Trine.

From the FIRST unto the SECOND where

EXAMPLE TWO:

Let's look at it with another pattern... simple squares. Imagine you have just throw the Numbers: 1, 5, 5, 4, 4, 6, 7 ...

STOP! 4.6.7 forms the first set of Three Different Numbers, Therefore the 4-6-7 is the TRINE. We place these details below, and show you the additions.

Throws	1st	2nd	3rd	4th	5th	6th	7th
Die throw	1	5	5	4	4	6	7
TRINE					4-6-7 Trine		
Additions		1+5=	6+5=	11+4=	15+4=	19+6=	25+7=
Summaries	1	6	11	15	19	25	32

Does this make sense? It is fairly straightforward, but if you don't quite get it yet, just go over things a few times. As with all things Pythagorean, when you see the pattern of things, it is self evident. Look up 1, 6, 11, 15, 19, 25 and 32 and see what "line" connects the numbers.

It is all about the Pythagorean process... All things Pythagorean follow lines of clear logic. If it does not, it is not Pythagorean. Everything you do must follow this same line of clear logic. What you have to do is to tune into this "Logic Line" and it will start to make sense.

These systems have been around for thousands of years. They DO work. As you attune yourself to them you will find that the Numbers will take on a life of their own. You may start seeing number combinations all around you. When you buy a VW, you suddenly see them all over the place. Likewise, number combinations will stand out for you.

A Golden Rule if you are to understand all this is to KEEP IT SIMPLE. Don't try to look into things too deeply. Trust your Intuition, ALLOW a picture to form. As you mentally make sense of the "Line of Number" allow your imagination to connect the dots. Remember "connect the dots" pictures you played with as a child? Let the picture form.

At some point, you start to see the whole picture take shape and you go "Oh, I get it now!" Like riding a bike, when you learn how, it is easy.

The THIRD must then Appear (Paracelsus)

Decimal Dice Workbook

VARIATIONS:

On the Following pages we offer some interesting Variations for using the 10 Sided Dice. Keep in mind, these are suggestions, and if you find some other way that works for you... Go for it. This Book is simply a signpost, not a post mortem.

REMEMBER: First, and always, ask a question or have something in mind you want to find an answer to.

Variation One: Looking for the TRINE.

Casting the Dice: Throw your 10 sided dice THREE TIMES. Do this until you have three different numbers in a single throw. (Note that any throw with a Zero is a no throw) The three different numbers form a TRINE. Look up what this means in the Trine Area of this book.

First Throw of 3	3	5	3	No Trine (Throw again)
Second Throw of 3	7	8	8	No Trine (Throw again)
Third Throw of 3	1	7	2	1-2-7 Trine ... Look it up!

Variation Two: Looking for the Composite

Casting the Dice: Throw the your 10 sided dice 3 x 3 times, add up all the numbers thrown. You are looking for a Composite Number. (Note: If the number is over 60, reverse it or add it down) EXAMPLE: Three Throws of Three: 3 - 8 - 2 / 4 - 7 - 9 / 1 - 5 - 8

3+8+2+4+7+9+1+5+8 = 47... 47 is the Composite Number so look it up, place the interpretation beside your question, and see what you can make of it. (Of course, you can also lay these numbers out in the Matrix Pattern, and see if there is anything in that for you as well)

If you arrive at a number higher than 60, try reversing it or Adding it bring it to a Number UNDER 60. For Example.
- 62 becomes 26.
- 78 cannot be reversed, so add it down to 15 (7+8 = 15)

Look up the interpretations for your number as a Composite Number and see how it offers an answer to your question. As a note, often the interpretation invites another question to be asked. If this is the case, follow through with the same procedure asking the new question.

Variation Three: Combinations of TWO Composites.

This variation requires you to interpret the interpretations. Here we are seeking to apply the Spiritual Law of Three by finding two Composites and then looking for the meaning behind the combination of the Two. It is an important variation to practice as this is really the key to your greatest success using Divinity Dice.

As always, ask a question before you throw. Casting the Dice: Take a 10 Sided Dice and throw it Five times, writing down the number throw each time. Consider the Zero as the number 10. Add these numbers but also the multiples of 12 to each number after the first throw, as in the following example: **You throw: 5, 10, 2, 7, 9**

1st throw	2nd throw	3rd throw	4th throw	5th throw	
5	10 (+ 12)	2 (+ 24)	7 (+36)	9 (+48)	
5	22	26	43	57	Composite

Write the numbers down as in the above example, and then do the additions as listed here:

1st throw	2nd throw	3rd throw	4th throw	5th throw	Total
5	10	2	7	9	5+10+2+7+9 = **33**
5	(+12) 22	(+24) 26	(+36) 43	(+48) 57	5+22+36+43+48 = 154 (1+5+4) = **10**

Keeping your question in mind, and look up the meaning for 33. Now, compare tis to the meaning for 10 in the Composite Number area. Between the meanings of these two numbers, a third idea or understanding will arrive.

Find the bridging point between the two Composite Numbers and you will find in the way this combines an answer to your question. You may need to look at this combination a few times over a number of days for

Decimal Dice Workbook

Variation Four: Group Method

This is a fantastic game to use with a group in order to help everyone come to agreement with some new direction or event. Any given group of people can get an answer to any question they may have by using Divinity Dice as an external tool. The benefit is two fold: It takes attention OFF the personality conflicts and onto a point of agreement, and secondly it gives people a sense of FUN. This is the secret combination to the lock within people's minds, take the attention of SELF and have some FUN. These two concepts combined open doors for resolution.

Often people get locked into a stalemate when it comes to communication and setting new goals. This is pretty normal for any group.

One way to break the "deadlock" is for each one of the members to take the 10 Sided Dice and throw it 3 to 6 times. Add up the numbers, and look up the Composite. This is "Your" number to contemplate on. Add the Composite down to the Fadic Number, and also contemplate on this. (You can also use the 20 sided dice here, if you have one)

It doesn't matter how large the group, when everyone has their own number to contemplate, discuss this for a little while. Now see what sort of agreement can be reached.

If no agreement can be reached, go to the next level. Sort out the different points of view into loose groups, there may only be two, or their may be several. Get people to sort themselves into groups where they feel they have an agreement. When the new groups are sorted, get them to add up "Their" numbers.

Add the Composite numbers of each person together in this new group, and reach the assembled addition of all the people, and add this down to a single number.

You will find opposition coverts to process, and process leads to solution. We "de-solve" issues into a solution via participation in the process.

Everyone discusses what number they all came down to, and from this point it can be remarkable how easily agreement can be reached.

Decimal Dice Workbook — *Find the Composite*

Why? Firstly, we have taken our attention off the problem, and put it on the solution. Secondly, we have shifted the Ego Self sideways... "We" are not being challenged to hold a point of View contrary to our belief. We are now invited (Via the casting of Dice) to invoke the Will of the Gods in the situation. This allows us to put our own wants and wishes to one side for a bit, and this alone lets more light into any situation.

There is a Third aspect that is a little more subtle... Everyone has agreed on SOMETHING, IE: The casting of the Dice. It may not seem like much, but everyone AGREED to do something in that group. This alone opens a doorway to resolution.

This method is subtle. It may not work right away, but if you come back tomorrow, you may find the solution is there for you no matter what the concern is. This is because you have asked people to put "themselves" and their issues aside for a moment, and to contemplate on Divine Guidance.

If you don't have dice, or this is too esoteric a thing for the people involved, get your folk to randomly select a passage from a sacred book, or some book you know everyone in that group respects. It is not as clear cut or as definitive as using the Dice, but the same principles apply.

The main thing is to find a point of agreement, where everyone can work around something that moves them outside of their personal view.

So, you have mastered these Game, and want MORE? Go to the official web pages at: www.divinitydice.com.au

The pair of dice shown at right was found at Herculaneum. The Romans called these *tesserae*, but they also had knucklebones with only four marked faces called *tali*.

The THIRD must then Appear (Paracelsus)

www.numberharmonics.org

Decimal Dice Workbook

INTERNET ENQUIRIES

You may make enquires and/or comments regarding this book and the information it provides via the internet. Go to **divinitydice.com,au** for Bulletin Boards, email addresses and further information..

Any advanced study courses and/or seminar information will be posted to this site. Of particular interest are the commercial pages of the Pythagorean Guild at www.numberharmonics.com

The author has devoted enormous time and effort towards resolving the Music Therapy and Sound Healing techniques of the Pythagorean schools. **Go to www.numberharmonics.org for more information about this remarkable advance in Pythagorean knowledge.**

Following Pages: Now we look at Composite Numbers. A thought to keep in mind as you go through these next pages is that your AGE is a Composite Number. EG: If you are 42 years old, take a look at the interpretation for the 42 to see one of the energies at work in this cycle of your life. Try it! Look it up and then think about what this year means for you. Consider about how the Interpretation applies to your current situation.

Divinity Dice

You like this book, and want MORE?

Great ... there is much so more you can learn about Dice. Go to the Divinity Dice study are begin to open up to all the OTHER areas of Dice interest.

To the left are the Five Platonic Solids, converted to Dice. These Dice are what we use in the main forms of Divinity Dice. The dice and book on how to use them can be found at:

www.divinitydice.com.au

From the FIRST unto the SECOND where
www.numberharmonics.org

Decimal Dice Workbook

COMPOSITE NUMBERS:
Where they came from and what they mean to You

For countless centuries mankind has sought to resolve the deeper aspects of the natural world in a way we can understand. As a race, we have tried to define life according to known and observable Laws and Principles. All the mysteries and ancient teachings were an attempt at making some sense of the "unknowable". This is the basis of all religion.

As a result, portent and meaning would be ascribed to the will of the Gods. Examples: The way Lightning strikes a tree. The manner in which a child draws first breath. These were all some of the various signs and events that might contain a hint of the Divine Will. The driving principle of many ancient teachings were that the Gods are trying to talk to us through these things, what we now call Omens.

All cultures in all times have attempted to describe a connection between the supernatural and the natural worlds. It devolves to superstition and dogma over time, but this religious principle, which is universal in Man, usually starts as a genuine need to know the truth. The Pythagoreans basic credo was "All is Number". A measure could be drawn against any living thing, if you understood which rule to apply. The Pythagoreans took a scientific approach and used the universal language of Mathematics to ascribe certain latencies and portents to natural phenomena.

Indeed, they saw "phenomena" as the earthly result of the Noumena, or the unformed Spiritual quality of life. The word "Numeral" comes directly from this word, as does Numinous.

The Pythagoreans took information from every culture, and in particular Mathematical Information. They then reformed this into a University Course for the modern world. They combined specific knowledge from a number of cultures to create a "gestalt" culture or teaching.

Pythagoras (and his techniques of theory then proof) started a wave of learning that created a transferable form of teaching that would survive the founder INTACT and FUNCTIONAL for some 1000 years. It is a truly extraordinary achievement. Even some terms that he coined are still in common use today. In fact, his entire system of teaching, his scientific philosophy and his astounding ability to find the common line between many cultures remains the basis for many Universities even to this very day. (not that many current Chancellors will admit it!)

The THIRD must then Appear (Paracelsus)

Decimal Dice Workbook

Composite Number Interpretations

1 ... One represents Logos or the singular creative spark. It says: Take Courage and start anew.

Be prepared for change. Also be prepared for unexpected gifts and blessings. Listen to what others say, but set your own course.

2... Two indicates the need to decide. The options are there, but where is your purpose, where is your best direction?

Make a stand for what is right. Consider your options, and then CHOOSE. Remember your ethics.

3... Three represents both Creativity and Planning. The suggestion is to look at the Goal as if it is already Achieved.

Go to the heart of the matter. Navigating the obstacles to get to the promised land does not really need 40 years in the desert.

4... When the Four is present you are being advised to look at the details yet also look out to the horizon as you consider them.

New horizons are being offered, but will you step forward with vigour and courage or retreat into conservative patterns?

5... Communication and Chaos are highlighted. Five is a Catalyst for change and new connections. It indicates that it is time to start a new project.

A primary message is: Look for the new opportunity. Time for change! **Time to Move On.**

How we see Change is important at this point. How you see, not what you see, will determine your actions in this coming cycle..

6... Six is the Scared Number of Intuition, Household Happiness, and also Enterprise. If you can combine these three elements, all you do will be successful.

How do you this? Practice listening to your Inner Voice. Remember patience is the virtue above all virtues.

7... The Dark Horse of Number is the Seven. Secret dreams, hidden desires and mystical perception all come together when this Number is awakened

The message here is, dig deeper into the body of your dreams and wishes, and find out what is driving them. Find out what is feeding your hidden needs and desires. Get to know yourself. Only then will you be set free from your sad self and the secret fears.

From the FIRST unto the SECOND where

www.numberharmonics.org

Decimal Dice Workbook   *Interpretations for Composites*

8... Reap the Harvest. What is in this moment that you can gather? Inspect the fruit, then prune the tree accordingly.

There is no free lunch. What you get in this cycle is what you have earned. (Good or Bad)

9... As one door opens, another closes. This is the Mantra of the Nine. Expect change to occur.

Understanding the process is not what is important here. DOING is what counts. Move on to the next stage. Let Go, and leave behind what is no longer useful. If you hang onto the past, you will miss the train.

10... Symbolized as the "Wheel of Fortune" a throw of TEN speaks of negative Karma as much as the lucky turn of the dice. Change is noted.

The difference between a positive outcome as opposed a negative is often to do with how you finish the last cycle. Follow the Law of Completion and all will work out well.

11... Decide your path. Walking the talk is where the learning comes, so ACT. Forget the words and get on with the actions.

The 11 signifies new possibilities, apprenticeship and a fresh start. Old projects may take fresh root in new and changing circumstances.

12... Signifies the completion of a task. Personal sacrifice and your freedom of speech may arise as issues. Find a way to Serve Life and you will discover your path to financial and inner freedom

You may go through difficulty but it will bring you to a point of greater clarity. Trust Life to look after the details and go for the end goal.

13... You may be greatly misunderstood at this time, but if you hold to your truth, all will be well.
This is not at all unlucky and indicates a new energy arriving in your life. This is often a message that CHANGE is happening, but which way will the change go? It is time to seek advice from someone you trust as regards your best direction.

14... Snakes and Ladders: A number of movement, travel and new associations.

14 is a very fortunate number. However, caution and prudence are advised, *especially in the choice of associates.* There is a simple rule when this number comes up... Do not have anyone in your immediate business surroundings who you cannot trust or who you cannot communicate with easily. Watch out for Snakes in the Grass.

The THIRD must then Appear (Paracelsus)   37
www.numberharmonics.org

Decimal Dice Workbook

15... The number of Magic and the Fay (fairy) folk. Be careful of your inner thoughts, for they will affect all around you. Your choices will attract Cornucopia or Disaster

15 will often indicate magic (consciously or unconsciously) at work behind the scenes. Trust that the dam is about to break, and make sure you are prepared for the entrance of the new.

16... Associated with the Tower of Babel. This is a warning to be aware of your Ego. Make sure it does not rule your heart.

Calamity will strike when you least expect it. Build carefully and well, be sure of your foundations, your associates and your intentions. Also make sure you have a buffer zone. Take an umbrella because it may soon be raining.

17... The Seventeen indicates that Soul will rise like the phoenix from all adversity, stronger and better for the trial.

Relax. Get to know yourself as you meet the changing circumstances of your lives. When your reactions and actions in life become housed in an attitude of open enjoyment, you will experience life in any number of new and interesting ways. Until then, this is a message that things are changing, and so be prepared.

18... This number is symbolic of the material nature seeking to conquer the spiritual.

Time to get rid of the Mortgage and focus on what really counts in your life. Have you spoken to your God this morning? Have you told your loved ones you care for them? Have you patted the dog? There are roses that need smelling right now!

19... Symbolized by the Sun. 19 is considered to be extremely fortunate for finance, self esteem and matters of honour.

This number indicates successful outcomes with all things associated with it. It is time to shine, so shine on you crazy diamond.

20... Recognized as "Judgment" It is a time of introspection towards yourself. Can you weigh a heart?

Look for a worthwhile purpose to fill this day. Let go of your concerns about what others may think or feel about you, and discover what it is you really want.

21... The Universe awaits. This represents achievement and honours. It is victory, but rarely is this easily won. 21 indicates victory after a long fight.

Would the Stars and moon judge you? No, so why judge yourself?

From the FIRST unto the SECOND where

www.numberharmonics.org

Decimal Dice Workbook

Interpretations for Composites

Get on with it, and live in the highest, lightest way possible.

22... The true Fool is the most intelligent person in the room. This represents a raw energy, and the person with it often likes to clown around, but behind the clown mask there is often a calculating and satirical nature.

View things with lightness and humour. Know that all things will pass. The time to act will soon arrive. Be prepared.

23... The Star. This number indicates assistance from higher forces. This can be divine guidance, or as mundane as receiving "jobs from the boys".

Even if you have been a complete no-hoper till now, the 23 can still trigger vast change and improvement in your circumstance. You will be favoured by someone higher up, and looked after in some way. Look to the Gods or your friends, or both! Can you hear the turn of the tide?

24... Self Sufficient Unto the Day. Your journey to freedom begins in this moment.

You must choose your own your destiny in this cycle. Your freedom to act is related directly to the depth of your fortitude. No one can be beholden to any man or thing and be happy with themselves at the same time.

25... A favourable period. It indicates strength gained through experience, and noble ideals becoming a practical wisdom.

The message is, focus on your goals. Set your sights into the practical framework of what can be achieved in each day, and go for it.

26... A number with the gravest warnings for the future. It foreshadows disaster by negative or ethically weak associations.

The message is, learn to love, but to also be careful who you love. Protect your reputation and stay out of "Gossip Circles".

27... Reward will come from the application of intellect, not physical force. The heart knows best.

The Message is to stay focussed and balanced in what you do. Practice patience with all things, and be kind to yourself. Trust to the Intelligence of your Heart in all things.

28... Query all that comes, and your good fortune will appear through this effort. An unfortunate number for the gullible.

This is a negative world, and that it must be dealt with accordingly.

Decimal Dice Workbook

When you grasp this notion, the 28 becomes very fortunate and you sail through the problems.

When you use your Negativity in a positive way things will work out for you. The Luck of Irish seems to follow you, and only you will know what effort you have put in to get to where you are. You KNOW you make your own luck.

29... Contrary 29 indicates both Deception and High Ideals. Trickery is possible here so look for hidden agendas from others. The shadows inside yourself may reveal a truth you never expected.

Move carefully and thoughtfully during this period. You must search your soul and discover your true inner desires if any lasting happiness is to be found

30... Thoughtful, deductive and contemplative. Excellent for the writer, scientist and explorer.

The effect of the 30 can be an elevated pattern of thought, but be aware that you can starve your own emotions from too much detachment. This can affect how you relate to others, and make simple conversation seem difficult. Despite this, people with the 30 energy often draw others to them, particularly when in support of a worthy cause.

31... This number can carry great power. It indicates influence over external events.
Your ability to communicate with others is what will open the door for you. The major lesson here is understanding Manipulation as a way to lie the truth. Be careful not to get lost in the learning.

32... A highly favourable number. A number of Magic and Freedom.

Excellent if you are working in the public arena. The 32 has a magical quality to it, and excepting the fact that it encourages "flash judgments" of others, it is generally a very carefree and positive vibration.

33... This number is known for the undertaking of a Higher Spiritual Learning. Do you feel something calling you?

The person affected by the 33 is often highly intuitive. Many suffer from over sensitivity as a result of this. Higher Learning is accented, in particular spiritual learning. The question to ask is "What is it that I really want? What do I need?"

34... Indicates strength gained through experience. Tend the Garden with care, and you will discover the secret herbs.

After a period of solitude, your spring will come, and the new

From the FIRST unto the SECOND where

www.numberharmonics.org

Decimal Dice Workbook — Interpretations for Composites

flowers of thoughts, feeling and expression will emerge. Writing is highlighted as your method of communication. Specifically, the message here is to record your dreams.

35... Excellent for money, learning and growth. However, you may experience poor judgement with personal relationships.

Look around and get a bigger view. If you are working in business selling Orange juice, you need to know all about your competitors products as well as your own if you wish to succeed. Do the market research.

36... This indicates strong character and high ideals.

This is a time for reflection, consideration and contemplation. As you build to the next level of your life, the Law of Silence must be applied. If you are to reach the highest level within yourself you will learn the Art of True Silence, which is found in knowing what to say at the right time and in the right place. There is often an intensity here which can create difficulties and problems behind the scenes.

37... In this cycle you can discover great freedom, or conversely, greater servitude to your own mind

Personal Confidence plays a big role is how quickly you develop your best aspects. It is important for you to get a good grounding in the basics of life if you are to get the best out of this cycle. Maybe consider taking a course or following up on some needed research before you move on.

38... There is a potent energy here, but it must be directed or things will collapse with confusion, anger and apathy. Be warned! Get focussed on the essentials

If you can get the 38 to work for you, it will work best down avenues of research, study and engineering. Once you have your confidence, however, many fields of endeavour and/or possibility will open up.

39... It is better to understand than to be understood.

Look to secure and clarify the relationships in your life. This is a warning sign. Beware the ties that bind. People may try to "own" you and tie you down with their beliefs. Snip it in the bud, and you will do better..

40... This indicates a time of self containment, and isolation to work out the inner questions.

This is a time of learning and growing inwardly towards your

Decimal Dice Workbook

goal. Like the seed in the soil, you are preparing for the spring. Pay attention to the small details around you and the larger picture will look after itself.

41... If you are practical and reliable, this period is often found to be extremely lucky.

You will generally excel with 'hands on' sort of work. Don't sweat the small stuff. Soldier on and the difficulties before you will fade away.

42... At Sixes and Sevens we discover the path is found in the addition of all that we have to hand.

There is trouble, but also a solution. You will find it in the elements that created the problem. Patience is also needed. The term "At Sixes and Sevens" applies here, and we need to learn the art of Silence until we grasp what the core issues are.

43... Upheaval and change lead to new learning.

Like the storm clearing the air, this number can appear to start a loud crash and thunder around you, but overall the result is a clearing. Obviously, if you are of a frail heart you will not find this energy pleasant, yet what can you do when the heavens create a storm? Find shelter, stay warm, and wait till it passes.

44... This can be a most unsettling and unpleasant energy. It indicates heavy karma and dealing with social conditions.

So often the "way" we approach people and situations is what determines a Positive or Negative outcome. It's not what you do here, but HOW you do that will show you your way. A hint for success! Break some rules, and discover your truth. See things in a new light, and that light will in turn shine on you, allowing others to see you differently. If this vibration is present, pick up your courage and go for life.

45... Silent and sure, you can continue under pressure in a way most people find astonishing.

This is a really positive energy that shines like the sun, yet all things have their opposite. In this period significant times of ill health, poverty and the worst sorts of betrayal can come about. Change can strike quickly and without warning, but be resilient. No-one is indestructible in a physical body, but with the 45 behind you, you may well come close.

46... Excellent for those who commit themselves to the project. Be aware that without a sense of purpose you are useless.

From the FIRST unto the SECOND where

www.numberharmonics.org

Decimal Dice Workbook   *Interpretations for Composites*

Even so, you will discover that your greatest joy comes from the well being and health of your heart, mind and body. You need a focus and a goal, but remember: In order to allow your Soul to shine more brightly you need to take care of yourself.

47... *Learn to Choose and your choice will lead you home. Love, but not necessarily marital love, is waiting for you.*

Stop looking for external conditions to solve your problems. What you need is already at hand. You just have to realize you can choose your path and you will be set free.

48... *This is one of the great numbers. Can you live up to it?*

There is a pulse or rhythm here that must be felt in the heart if you are to meet the challenges this number presents. It takes a good deal of inner courage to succeed when this energy is present.

49... *An odd, quirky period is coming up for you. You will attract odd, quirky personalities.*

Life seems an unbalanced force, but like a dissonance in music, a person can draw great energy from the difficulty in creating harmony. Naturally, this takes a Master Musician... Are you prepared to really master the social and emotional elements of your life? A suggestion: Always do a little bit more than is necessary, and it will serve you well.

50... Look for the element of Surprise in your life.

A wicked humour or sarcastic streak that put you at odds with gentle folk can now be made more harmonious. As maturity comes a desire for peace and harmony may cause you to grow past a need to burst bubbles, and soften to a clear observation of life. In the next 6 month period you may look back and, seeing the changes, wonder if you are the same person

51... *The warrior. A very potent number, indicating sudden and unexpected advancement.*

If you can learn your own limits, yet test the edges of your experience, you will be able to go beyond them and find great joy in this life. If you cannot, the energy of the 51 will tend to stay in the background, and not really work for or against you.

52... *Bring your focus of thought and action inward upon the self.*

To fully be a part of life, you need to learn the difference between the natural state of your being, and the social animal that has been trained into you. A period of reflection and contemplation every day will help you know yourself better. Man, know thyself.

The THIRD must then Appear (Paracelsus)   43

www.numberharmonics.org

Decimal Dice Workbook

53... An Important Cycle. This is a time of Harvest and Manifestation, but if you break the Law of Silence all will reverse.

The Law of Silence is more about knowing what to say, and when to say, rather than just not speaking. It takes a degree of focus and awareness to maintain this knowing. If you can reach this state, this is a powerful, spiritually and financially fruitful period for you.

54... Reaching the Stars requires letting go of the Earth.

Will you dare to break your personal boundaries? Can you go past the social norms, and discover the real desires that are the "You" in you?

Can you brave your own shadows? Will you seek to express self in whatever way you must? Or will you hold fast to your fears? Go forward, or go backwards...

55... Your Greatest Good is your Highest Aspiration

The 55 indicates a path to follow. The first step on any path is the decision to start, while the second step is continuing to walk the path. (Which requires strength of purpose and balancing of inner dreams with the physical world) The third step is either more of the same, or Spiritual Learning. We can cycle on the first two steps for a whole lifetime, but eventually we come to spiritual learning just by getting worn down by experience.

The forth step then arrives. This is learning to go beyond the barriers of other people's expectations, and it is a very tricky step.

Finally we arrive at the Fifth Step... This is where we come to understand that our deepest aspirations, hopes and wishes will always be something which serves the greatest good. So... Where are you on this journey?

56... Loosening the bowstring allows the arrow to fly

Look up at Orion in the Night sky. He is one of the few constellations that is visible from all hemispheres. Are you allowing yourself to be visible? Are you allowing others to see the real you? Can YOU see you? It is already set up for you, so why do you hesitate? It is time to trust life will support you.

57... The Heights are the Lows, the Ins are the outs AND Vice Versa.

Your associations will define much of your experience in this cycle. If you are in the gutter with the drunks, emotionally or mentally, you will either continue this OR take the opportunity for change that now presents itself. A scandal will soon break that will cause you concern.

From the FIRST unto the SECOND where

www.numberharmonics.org

Decimal Dice Workbook Interpretations for Composites

58… As Opium is gold to the Addict, a smile is gold to a child

What is it that you value? What is it that sets your heart dancing? Find you path to freedom through knowing what gives you true joy. Always, trust that the secret message of Life is "Freedom, Joy, and Sharing"

59… The rainbow is only half a circle, and it shifts according to how you see it.

In this period, you must use your imagination to see the hidden sides of your own nature. In this cycle you can find deeper and deeper insights into your heart and mind.

60… Can you hear the Call to the Highest Within?

When he crossed the Rubicon, Julius Caesar shouted "Let the dice fly high!" You have made your decisions and now your destiny is put into the winds of change. All that follows is a result of your preparation, your instincts, and the trust and friendships you have built up to this date. There are no half measures, there is no pulling back, you must play out your fate as best you can.

Close of Composite Section

The Six Box Game:

This is a quick and simple little Game to practice. Throw the 10 sided die three times, and write the numbers down in the box as shown to the right.

Add the First and Second die to get a Composite. Then add the Second and Third die to get a Composite.

Finally add these two additions to get the third and final addition.

Read the interpretations in the Composite Number section, and there you have it.

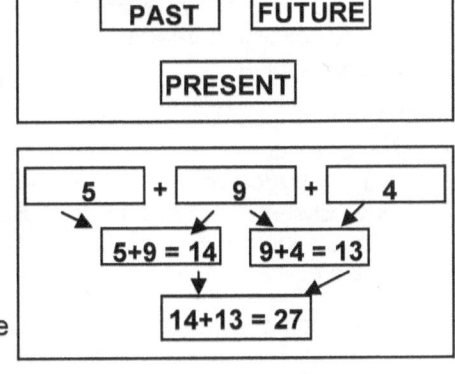

The relative positions for the Past Future and Present are shown. This game gives you an idea of where your question comes from, where it is right now, and where it is going. You will find it to be surprisingly accurate for such a simple game. Play with it at parties, and surprise your friends!

The THIRD must then Appear (Paracelsus)

Decimal Dice Workbook

TRINES: History and Background

The Eighty-Four (84) Pythagorean Trines are little known, yet extremely powerful Number Combinations. Even though Pythagoras is most famous for his mathematical Theorem based on a Triangle, there is a little information available on the subject of Trines and the Pythagoreans. In one 18th Century manuscript a distinct mention was found of these sacred elements of Pythagorean thought, but it was not until a Roman Temple (based on the Pythagorean Teachings) was discovered in late 1991 that the real nature of the Pythagorean Trines was fully realized. Other than this and the 18th Century manuscript reference you will find precious little information on Pythagorean Trines out side of this book or The Book of Number.

What is a Trine? In simple terms, it is any combination of three numbers. In the aspect of the Pythagorean Matrix any combination of three numbers forms what we call a Trine. They are significant, and based on the same Harmonic Structures as Western Music. In the Decimal System there are Eighty-Four (84) non-repeating combinations.

The Pythagoreans held that Harmonic Music was a form of divine truth. In particular, the Inner Music, or Shabda was focussed on. This "Tone" was called "the Music of the Spheres" and the name has survived millennia. The term describes the Celestial Sound Current. Do you ever hear that odd High Pitched sound in or around your ears? This is the whisper of the Spirit in our ear, and it often comes as a high pitched Vowel Tone. This "Music" is very real. Many people report hearing it, though few are conscious of what it means, or what they can do with it. It is the Universal "White Noise".

The high pitched humming or buzzing that comes in or around your ears on odd occasions is a deep spiritual truth manifesting itself. As mentioned, the Pythagoreans called it "The Music of the Spheres". Socrates called it the "Ekstasis" (where the verb Ecstasy comes from) and the Ancient Greeks just tended to refer to "it" as the "E" (as it is often heard to sound like a drawn out "E" vowel tone)

The pitch and quality of these various Tones were identified and categorized according to Number. Specific combinations of Tone were noted to emanate from people who had specific character traits, and over time these too were catalogued. It is important to note that these Trines are omnipresent and pervasive.

From the FIRST unto the SECOND where

Decimal Dice Workbook

That is to say, all combinations of all tone exists simultaneously at all points in time and space, BUT, and here is the connection with Divinity Dice, when the right combination of events occurs, it is like inserting the right Key into the lock. We now can open an inner door.

Like unlocking a safe and finding out what has been stored in there, we dial up a certain combinations of number, and this leads us to a specific door. Through that door and inside the room there are a specific set of conditions we are about to walk into.

The Mathematics of Harmonics is VERY specific. We can prove the scientific principles but the subtle inner truths are, in a word, non-provable (other than by personal experience). However, experience over millennia tells us that specific combinations of Number mean specific thing. The way this interacts with you will vary. and this is what is determined by the random throwing of the Dice.

You have your OWN harmonic signature. The interaction between yourself and what comes up with the throwing of the Dice is what matters. Not just the Numbers … Your interpretation of what unfolds is what counts. There is ALWAYS a message in the random casting of the Dice for you. Rarely do you receive something that you expect, and often the interpretation leads you to other questions and further understandings of what you are asking about.

That is how it is with questions and answers. The two are a little like waves interacting in a wave pool, they can build and accent the energy of each other with a greater peak, or the two can cancel each other out, with little effect being noted.

The facts remain that no one can fully determine what each aspect and shade of meaning that a specific combination creates. There are literally millions and millions of combinations that are possible. Approximately 43 million possibilities, in fact. Obviously, no book can come even close to containing all of these potentials. Even so, all the basic aspects have been resolved and tested in field work for over 25 years and the basic interpretations you will find are sufficient. We still find more shades of meaning every year, of course. No one wants to wait another 1000 years so we decided to run with the latest and clearest definitions.
We ask you to realize a simple truth. It is how you INTERACT with an interpretation that s important. Not the interpretation of itself, but how it fits you personally.

The THIRD must then Appear (Paracelsus)

www.numberharmonics.org

Decimal Dice Workbook

This is what is important here. We all have so many shades and variations to our characters that even with our own interpretations things will change. Different understandings will be evoked at different times, and we just have to run with what seems right at the time.

Some things you read may even seem to oppose your experience. If a particular aspect says "This energy is considered Lucky" but your life to date has been anything but lucky, it may be that it is all about to turn around OR maybe the suggestion is that you have a subconscious sabotage mechanism blocking the natural flow? These are the harder things to work out when throwing the Dice.

It will surprise you. After 25 years of experience I still find I get surprised at how a new combination of influences will add up to such a clear, to the point PERSONAL reading that answers the question.

Early in my study I came across a stubborn German who refused to believe in anything other than what he could see and touch. I was in a coffee shop, and it got out that I read Number Patterns, so he demanded I read his. Well, in his life he had gone through four name changes, had moved all over the world, and so he had lots of "pivotal" dates to draw patterns from.

In traditional Pythagorean Number Theory, Dates are viewed as a series of cycles,. These cycles are broken down to their "bones" to reveal patterns. Any Pattern or sequence that repeats is important.

It took 4 hours, and he sat there stone faced as I read WHEN he likely changed his name, WHERE he likely changed his name, and the conditions around which the name changed. He gave no hint as to right or wrong until I had finished. Yet, when it was over he said "It is impossible! How could you have known EVERYTHING about me from just NUMBERS!" I said it wasn't me, but his numbers that told the story. I just read them. (I didn't tell him that I was more surprised than he was, of course! We must keep some things secret.)

What we have done with Divinity Dice is to shift the focus from Dates and "universal" number patterns to the random casting of Dice. We have had to rearrange the meanings to reflect this. I ask you to remember, nothing is so complete that another shade of meaning will not be possible. What you have here is more than enough to work with, however.

Even though there is a high degree of flexibility with interpretations, the basic framework of the number combinations is very defined. Things can change INSIDE the box, but the shape of the box is what it is.

From the FIRST unto the SECOND where

www.numberharmonics.org

Decimal Dice Workbook

A very important note: Always remember that things can REVERSE in their meaning. If the exact opposite of what is being described by your throw of the Dice is occurring in your life, then don't be surprised. It happens because we have Free Will. The interpretations merely indicate a possibility, and often people have gone past that "zone" or Energy Field. You may be opposing the process, or avoiding it. Either way, you will get a clue with what the Dice turn up.

How to work with a reversal. If the interpretation that seems opposite to your experience: Simply ask the dice more on the subject. Is it good for you or otherwise? If otherwise, then we must ask what attitude or what focus of attention we need to develop in order to bring things back on track. This is called being open to Change.

More than anything, the ability to change your mindset and your pre-set emotional charges will enhance your quality of life. The Dice Games are specifically intended to assist you in this area.

The Trines describe powerful forces that exist in the substrata of existence. they are by no means the ONLY area of Pythagorean Thought, but they were the area most easily applied to divination with Dice. We have courses out that describe the full Pythagorean System of Number Analysis if you care to take your understanding of this area further.

Go to www.numberharmonics.org for more details.

PYTHAGORAS:

Pythagoras of Samos: A leading Light of the Philosophy Movement in the Golden Age of Greece. His teaching covered many areas, specifically Mathematics and Numerology, but also he originated many other disciplines, such as: Topography Mapping, Surveying and Engineering.

Famous for the "Pythagorean Theorem" this is paradoxically one thing he never invented. He merely demonstrated the Proof of its working, and yet in doing so, Pythagoras developed the "Observation and Proof" method of modern scientific discovery.

Decimal Dice Workbook

Index to Trines.

Throw the 10 Sided Die, and look up the relevant Trines. That's all there is to the Game. Simple, Easy, and to the Point.

TRINE			PAGE	TRINE			PAGE	TRINE			PAGE
1	2	3	52	2	3	4	66	3	5	8	80
1	2	4	52	2	3	5	66	3	5	9	80
1	2	5	53	2	3	6	67	3	6	7	81
1	2	6	53	2	3	7	67	3	6	8	81
1	2	7	54	2	3	8	68	3	6	9	82
1	2	8	54	2	3	9	68	3	7	8	82
1	2	9	55	2	4	5	69	3	7	9	83
1	3	4	55	2	4	6	69	3	8	9	83
1	3	5	56	2	4	7	70	4	5	6	84
1	3	6	56	2	4	8	70	4	5	7	84
1	3	7	57	2	4	9	71	4	5	8	85
1	3	8	57	2	5	6	71	4	5	9	85
1	3	9	58	2	5	7	72	4	6	7	86
1	4	5	58	2	5	8	72	4	6	8	86
1	4	6	59	2	5	9	73	4	6	9	87
1	4	7	59	2	6	7	73	4	7	8	87
1	4	8	60	2	6	8	74	4	7	9	88
1	4	9	60	2	6	9	74	4	8	9	88
1	5	6	61	2	7	8	75	5	6	7	89
1	5	7	61	2	7	9	75	5	6	8	89
1	5	8	62	2	8	9	76	5	6	9	90
1	5	9	62	3	4	5	76	5	7	8	90
1	6	7	63	3	4	6	77	5	7	9	91
1	6	8	63	3	4	7	77	5	8	9	91
1	6	9	64	3	4	8	78	6	7	8	92
1	7	8	64	3	4	9	78	6	7	9	92
1	7	9	65	3	5	6	79	6	8	9	93
1	8	9	65	3	5	7	79	7	8	9	93

From the FIRST unto the SECOND where

www.numberharmonics.org

Decimal Dice Workbook

INDEX to TRINE INTERPRETATIONS:

In this section, the Interpretation of Trines you can look up the combination of three numbers in the column to the left. This refers you to the page where the interpretation for this Trine can be read.

Please note that all interpretations must be read with consideration for other aspects that come up in your use of Divinity Dice. Each aspect changes the focus of the interpretation. More than this, each changing aspect will offer you a way to modify your questions and your understanding of the answers.

Getting to your answer and even getting you're your "truest" question is a little like peeling an onion. Every layer peels back to another layer, and sometimes it gives you tears.

What you are entering into when you start the Divinity Dice is a process. You may well be quite content with the basic answer you get from using one of the Forms in the book, or it may spur you onto to ever greater thoughts and considerations.

You are not alone on the journey. However this process works for you, be assured that the path you tread has been walked many times by many people over the centuries. It only looks like the Road Less Travelled because you are the only one here at the moment.

Working with the Index is somewhat obvious. When you get your combination of Three Different Numbers from the various throws of the Decimal Dice, come to this page and it will refer you to the page where your interpretation is. EG: 2-4-9 Trine is on Page 109.

The rest is simply following and understanding what is written, and then applying this to your personal situation. This reduced section for Trine Interpretations is for the Decimal Dice book only ... The full interpretations are to be found in the primary book on Divinity Dice.

We wish you the best on this next stage of your journey with the Dice.. In the words of the ancient blessing: May your Intuition (Inner Voice) guide you well

Interpretations for Trines — **Decimal Dice Workbook**

1-2-3 Trine: Plan your Day, arrange your life, but even so you must allow the fates their passage

The One –Two -Three aspect of this Line of Force almost speaks for itself. This Trine speaks of planning, of creative endeavour. It applies as much to organizing the house budget as running the country, or even to writing a poem. However, are you planning things to death? The rule here is to simply organize a things to the point where it starts to takes on a life of its own. Be aware and sensitive to this.

This is a methodical aspect, and people affected by this Trine generally do not like interference of any sort. Yet so we often find that plans and hopes go wrong without the input and advice of others to help our focus. Part of the learning that comes with this aspect is to keep your own counsel, yet listen to what others have to say.

The message is, go for it. You will have the desire to create SOMETHING, so just go do it. Your Motto is: *Build and they will come.*

1-2-4 Trine: One coin well spent is worth a thousand coins dreamed.

This is a practical Trine. When it occurs you are being told two things... Mind your P's and Q's and yet don't be too confined by the patterns of your past. It is a fortunate aspect for money, but not for Love... At least not until you allow your more Avant-garde "self' out of the bag

However, not many can go past their personal barriers. In this case the effect of this Trine tends to make you insular. Do feel a need to hoard things, be it money, ideas or possessions? If this is happening it indicates you are being closed to new ideas and interactions with others. Potlach... Throw it away! Get yourself free!

Stop using "things" to protect you from a one to one connection with life. Try writing poetry and recording your dreams. Use this as a way out of your own "mind trap" and as a release from the internal pressures you feel. This is a positive outlet for you, but go further. Get some exercise. Get fit both mentally and physically..

Your Motto is Thoreau's: *Better a live Dog than a Dead Lion*

From the FIRST unto the SECOND where
www.numberharmonics.org

Decimal Dice Workbook

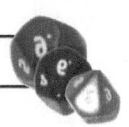

1-2-5 Trine: Success, Communication and Beauty create Grace. Fear creates the Opposite.

You are being presented with an opportunity to grow personally and spiritually, and often financially here. But your choice is simple. Are you moving forward with Love, or retreating with Fear You will be called to face yourself in the next cycle.

You will do well to trust your intuitive "leaps in the dark" when looking for solutions to problems. Even if if your choices appear to have not worked, doorways will have opened and soon enough a solution will come. Are you finding you need a lot of time alone? This is the energy of this Trine at work. It is part of the maturing phase of the cycle. Often when others call you "difficult" it is simply you thinking through your internal process. At the end of things, however, there is usually a flower that emerges to advertise the work of the plant.

Be patient with yourself. Your Motto is: *Make way for the King... And let 'me' through while you are at it.*

1-2-6 Trine: Strike a Match and See the Light.

It is so obvious, but few people see the simple truth. If you are in the dark, strike a match. The "Match" is many things: Trusting your instincts, Believing in Self Understanding that YOU are the lamp holder. The fire in the lamp symbolizes several things. Firstly, the light pierces the darkness. Secondly, the raw flame clears the air of foul odour.

Thirdly, the flame is contained even as it remains open and visible. If you can see how these three aspects can combine in yourself you will have solved the unspoken riddle of this Trine.

Intuition and practicality combine to make this a very fortunate Trine, but you have to keep yourself in balance. If you have a tendency towards extremes in just about anything, then your luck will turn, and life will turn into some strange alley ways.

Your Motto is: *Life comes from Life. All things of God are borne of themselves, all things of Man are born of conflict and struggle.*

Interpretations for Trines **Decimal Dice Workbook**

1-2-7 Trine: Cast off the Fear and Fly. Be Brave. Reveal your Hidden Shadows to Yourself.

A powerful creative urge stalks this Trine. Creative yes, but with many insecurities and doubts that tend to block the natural flow. If you cannot rise above this in this cycle, you may alternatively find that you are drawn to supporting artists and writers in some way.

It is a substitute for your real feelings, but maybe you really weren't meant to be a starving artist or suffering poet role model in this lifetime. Most with this aspect will hold an interest in the arts. You will do well in cultural positions as you will have a resonance and sensitivity which enables you to recognize the finest art.

Alternatively, there is a "dark" calling here, with a desire for magic and influence that is calculated and manipulating. Choose well the path you walk: Your Motto is: *Whether you take the high road or the low road, focus on the destination.*

1-2-8 Trine: Why does the King of the Ocean Rule? Because He Rules from Below.

The above is from the I Ching: Why does the King of the Ocean Rule? He understands the process, and rules from inside it. This Trine is telling you to take charge of the various currents inside yourself. Understand where they go, what mood they create, and learn to work with the natural flows of your inner self. It is a contemplative yet active energy with a power that stems from patience and observance.

Even so, this is a practical, money orientated Trine. Be careful of being too easily be influenced by current trends. You like fashion, the stage, the latest electronic gimmicks, but are you really able to afford these? This is an interesting cycle, because money is something you don't just want, you really appreciate it! The lesson is to rule from below and you will find the money flows to you more easily

Overall it is fortunate. You are set to break through to a "New You" and this necessarily involves weathering the odd storm. Your motto is: *I sink therefore I swim*

Decimal Dice Workbook

1-2-9 Trine: Question 101... Are you a Cowering Mouse or a Creative Lion?

So... Are you going to take charge of your life, your imagination, your dreams? Are you going to work towards the goal, or sit and worry about the fears?

In this Trine we find many influences. There is a dreaming energy that likes to deal with concepts, especially when they are to do with beauty and form. When developed this gives a certain architectural sense to you. This is a Trine that likes to build, to create, to form something new from the clay of the past. So it may be that it is time to start a new building project. But be warned, the inherent fragility of the creative burst tends to make the energy here a little unstable.

You have two choices, make your dreams a reality or accept the lesser fate of having your dreams separated from your reality. It's your choice. Your Motto is: *Much gathers More. Less Gathers Loss.*

1-3-4 Trine: Lift your Heart with a Love for your Journey and then the burden will seem slight.

The energy of this Trine alters dramatically as you get older, either in years or in wisdom. This is one of the very few influences with this characteristic. As we grow older in Spirit, as well as in age we can learn to move with the rhythm of Time and Space about ourselves. This feeling has a sort of "breath" which, if you can tune into it, will awaken your sense of creativity which will in turn help solve your worldly concerns. This attitude requires a particular state of mind. Have you seen the way a child can become completely absorbed in its play, and will forget the passing of hours and the outside world? That is the state of mind you need to aim at.

To achieve this you will need to train your Imaginative and this is best done through a form of creative application. The nature of this creativity can take of many forms and is not necessarily limited to the traditional ideas of the arts. Get creative if you want to be free.

Your Motto is: "We thrive despite our shortcomings" Thoreau wrote this, and it fits well here.

The THIRD must then Appear (Paracelsus)

Interpretations for Trines   **Decimal Dice Workbook**

1-3-5 Trine: I Cherish, I Love, I Burn for you ... but be careful as I can be Fragile.

Trines like this generally invoke a conflict. It is a little like Helen of Troy not being happy with her circumstance and running off with her lover, uncaring of the circumstances or fates that will be called into play. Honesty is called for. Be honest with yourself. This Trine has a markedly different effect between the male and the female. With the Man it tends to cultivate a "girlish" sense while with the Woman it tends to make somewhat of a dreamer. As you get in charge of the energy, however, you develop excellent communication skills.

This Trine does tend to stir up conflict, but usually this is more awkward than painful. You have a fire inside you, and you have three choices. Let it burn like a wild fire, use the fire as a weapon, or contain your flame in a lamp. Or you can burn yourself up as a forth option. Beware the choices you make, that is the message.

Your Motto is a curious one: *The brighter the flame, the longer the shadows cast. Can you see your shadow comes from your light?*

1-3-6 Trine: Do you Hear the Harmony about you? Spread your wings and fly.

This is one of the most attractive Trines in the Noumenal Order. It is exceptionally harmonious, and if you are blessed with this Trine you are fortunate. This aspect calls up charm and wit, and will draw people to you. However, this can make for a devil as easily as it does a saint, and so you must always be careful to look at your motivations and desires. What is your true intention? What is your true Desire? This trine is also telling you to look at your heart, in order to discover what motivates you.

Do you hear that High Pitched Tone in or around your ears? This Trine is telling you to focus on this energy, and bring it into your heart. This is "The Music of the Spheres" ... But remember that we still have duties to fulfil, and don't neglect the physical for the pursuit of the spiritual. Your Motto is curious: *Life is telling me the way to go. Don't just listen to the message, ACT on it. Don't just float, FLY.*

From the FIRST unto the SECOND where
www.numberharmonics.org

Decimal Dice Workbook

1-3-7 Trine: *Alone but not Lonely.*

Are you looking for achievement in some form of artistic endeavour? This is a good aspect for you. However, this also indicates a period of sorrow and difficulty, and perhaps a time isolation while bringing this about. There often is a fear of failure looming about this Trine, and you may feel "haunted" at times. There is often a sense of being "pushed" or "driven" by the energy here. You feel the need to be alone but it will quite sharply conflict with your need for society. This is the test of the Social Consciousness. This Trine is saying "You must learn to stand joyfully alone". When you get this attitude, the Trine invokes a manifesting energy, and our dreams come true..

A clue: When our fear of failure is mastered it becomes a keystone in our success. We all have insecurity, it comes in waves, but do you surf these waves, or drown? "How does this work?" you may well ask. Doubt, fear and paranoia may well tell you what others are thinking, but at all times remember not to fear this influence

Simon and Garfunkel sang "I am a rock, I am an Island" ... But you are a part of life. Your Motto is: *Trusting Self means Trusting Life.*

1-3-8 Trine: *Be wary of Gifts and Promises and great Dreams. There is usually a Hidden Cost.*

This is a powerful aspect. Under its influence you may gain insight into the ways of mankind. This Trine combines the "Law of Three's" (manifestation) with the concept of Harvest (reaping what you sow). Secret dreams and hidden agendas can come to light in this cycle. The Gypsy Curse/Blessing "May you live in interesting times" is yours today.

You may find yourself at a crossroads of choosing either moral or immoral behaviour. You may come to understand "amoral" is closer to truth. All in all, this is a powerful aspect where much that is Positive OR Negative can come from the events of your life.

Give yourself the room internally to be yourself, and all will be well. Consider others but don't be too affected by the tribe. Go your own way. Your Motto: *Look that Gift horse in the mouth.*

The THIRD must then Appear (Paracelsus)

www.numberharmonics.org

Interpretations for Trines **Decimal Dice Workbook**

1-3-9 Trine: *Your Journey to Freedom begins with Integrity, Dignity and Self sufficiency.*

The focus here is on individuality and responsibility. The essential elements for attaining and maintaining our individuality is a sense of Identity (One), an ability to Create (Three), and the Power to Realize this (Nine). Without Integrity, Dignity and Self Sufficiency you will never find your power.

For some a really "mad" energy runs through this aspect. If so, few will understand you. There is an old saying: Expect to be misunderstood, expect difficulty, and you will rarely be disappointed..

Seeking ourselves in external events never really works... Sitting still, and finding some purpose to our life will allow the obvious to emerge. This is your only true path. When in doubt ask: *At the close of my life, will I be happy or sad if I do this?* But don't be a quiet little mouse, staying at home, obeying rules. If so: Stop that NOW. Go out and play up. Even so, the Motto remains: *The Millwheels of the Gods Grind Slowly, but Exceedingly Fine.*

1-4-5 Trine: *Be not so practical that ye cannot Love. Be not so Loving that ye cannot Hunt.*

Those affected by this Trine are often perceptive and angular. Do you like to find a side to an argument that is quite lateral? Do you like to "deal" in buying and selling all sorts of things? It suits you and you will make a passable living from this. It is not so much the money, but the thrill of the chase that can drive the energy of this Cycle. It is a Hunter, with the sharpened wit, pointed observation and barbed comment weapons.

Is this you? You may read this and think you are the OPPOSITE of this. If so, this Trine is telling you that this is something you need to develop. You need to be more of the Hunter than the Gatherer in this cycle. In another view, the Trine is saying that being active is what is needed now. Get off the couch and stop watching TV. When you pass from this world, will you have done something worthwhile?

Be pro-active and Go for it. Your Motto is: *Do not bear Fools Gladly!* And yet remember, sometimes the Fool has a useful message.

Decimal Dice Workbook

1-4-6 Trine: Be Open to the Truth. Trust you Heart, yet Test your Heart.

What is it that you want? This is the starting point for all people with this trine. Often you will be drawn back to memories of earlier years when this Trine is called up, and there are many "hidden" secrets they may be revealed. Things from your Childhood may come up, both positive and negative, that need to be "dis-charged" from your consciousness ... Always remember, your memory is coloured from the view of that Child. This is often a "clean out the attic" period of past emotions and unresolved thoughts.

Auspicious and fateful, this Trine indicates great success in the field of your choosing. Here you will depend largely on yourself, and often succeed beyond your own expectations Alternatively, you may go the opposite side of the sandwich, and become extremely unmotivated financially and uncaring about appearance ... Two ends of the same stick of ambition. Your Motto is one of positive Surrender: *If not this, Oh Lord, then something better.*

1-4-7 Trine: Your Reality is what You Expect. Are you Deciding what to Expect?

Are you taking charge of your Life? Are you making the decisions, and working towards the specific goals? It's time to sort out your life. You must KNOW what you want, because only then you will open up to the ways to achieve it. Even so, the Lesson of this energy is "Expect the Unexpected" Change will shake the ground when this Trine turns up

This Trine is suggesting "Leave the door of possibility open". Even so, many times we find this Trine called up when people are sitting in their Negatives. In this case, it will push you in ways that may hurt. Change is like giving birth ... Usually a painful experience.

Create Inner and Outer Space you need at this point. You value your freedom, and demand respect... but give others their fair share of freedom as well, and things will work out OK for you.

Your Motto is: *Not my will, but thine, oh Lord. (and do what you will)*

The THIRD must then Appear (Paracelsus)

Interpretations for Trines   **Decimal Dice Workbook**

1-4-8 Trine: Dedication to a Higher Goal. Take care with Investments.

This can be very unpleasant Trine on a personal level, but one that can be very good for business. The energy here can be very determined and uncompromising. "Get the job DONE". Is the attitude. Ideally you should learn to have the very basic and uncompromising attitude of this Trine when you go to work, but turn it off when you come home. It can be done, but grasping this "Off-On" thing can be very difficult.

Some under this aspect can be real pigs, but this may be what is needed for the project to be completed on time. If this is a part of your nature you will be a valuable foreman or CEO., but turn it off when you get home. Take care with Diet and Stress issues.

This Trine may be a warning to pull out of the Stock Market, or to trim back on the overheads. There is a "priest" in you which may hear a higher calling after you have cemented your position in the world. You will serve faithfully in whatever the cause that calls you. Your Motto is simple: *A thing worth doing, is worth doing well.*

1-4-9 Trine: The Warrior must Sharpen the Sword... But remember it cuts both ways!

This Trine has a powerful "Mover and Shaker" energy. It is like a bulldozer. Under this "Jupiterian" influence you want something done, you want it done NOW, and you do not want excuses. Of course, in real life, we have to be diplomatic, but when this Trine occurs it is saying "This is a time to push things through". There is a certain attitude you can pick up where even bad mechanics realize it would not be worth their while doing a bad job on your car. Because of this the job gets done right. Demand Value and forget the Mr Nice Guy, in other words.

If you have the 1-4—9 Trine in your life, it may be saying "Forge Ahead NOW" OR the opposite … It may be a warning to not push the boundaries and to look at the lay of the land before making decisions. There is a new horizon, but which road? In this cycle, make sure you give members of your family plenty of lee way. If you can manage this, a great peace will come upon those who possess this Trine. Your Motto: *If you can see it, it can be done.*

From the FIRST unto the SECOND where

www.numberharmonics.org

Decimal Dice Workbook

1-5-6 Trine: Make Kindness your Virtue and your Practice "Knowledge is not Virtue. Virtue is not Wisdom." (Ancient Egyptian Saying)

Is it True? Is it Necessary? Is it Kind? Ideally this is the motto you constantly employ. If you can use and practice this, you will find this Trine is an excellent aspect for the contemplative Soul. Practice random acts of unasked for Kindness. The energy, if you work with it, will help you to come into balance with your natural need for Love and your need for expression, whatever this may be for you.

In fact, what IS your natural Love and Expression? Guilt and repression are pandemic in our society and you need to see where these things affect you. Few really know what their natural needs are.

The Major Lesson here is one of learning to quieten the mind. You are aiming for a greater Intelligence of the Heart. Your Motto is: *It is only with the Heart that one sees rightly.*

1-5-7 Trine: A Paradox... Can you understand? Learning to be You requires a Loss of Yourself.

Have you seen how a Child will lose itself in Play? This is the image you need to hold before you when this Trine comes up. You need to connect to that sacred childlike space where a direct connection with the divine self and your inner awareness can occur. In the fields of your imagination there is a touchstone that makes everything real ...

This Trine is saying "Look for the Touchstone." Find the Sacred in YOU. Take a good look at your life, apologize and repair where needed, and then move on to better things.

Your emotions and your Identity can feel very challenged when this Trine appears. Often the message of this Trine is: Get ready for change. It may also indicate that someone is about to arrive who will be a catalyst in your life. Listen to your heart, and see what comes.

Your Motto tends to be: *Stick it under the rug.* Your Motto SHOULD be: *Don't should on me. (Pun intended)*

Interpretations for Trines   **Decimal Dice Workbook**

1-5-8 Trine: Strengthen Your Inner Resolve. Awaken the Fire in Your Heart.

In an ideal situation, you would be surrounded by all the books of the best writers, playing chess with Princes, and sipping Chartreuse while lounging in a Bedouin tent beside an Oasis near the Pyramids of Egypt. But, for some reason, things are not quite that way for you. The romantic dream is rarely the physical reality. The facts of the matter is, your dreams are generally in ruins by the time your pull up this Trine, and it will already be time to start again.

Read Humpty Dumpty. You are the egg, the king, all the king's horses AND you built the wall you fell off. You created the problem. Now you need to get out of the duct tape business, and into re-moulding Easter eggs. Strengthen your Inner Resolve and go for it.

There is a Karmic influence and yet also a calming sense of connection with life. In all, it is a bit of a puzzle box we need to work through. Your Motto is: *Alone but not lonely.*

1-5-9 Trine: Success comes to the patient ones, but don't wait around! Plan for Success.

SUCCESS! Your boat has finally come in, but are you on it? Did you remember to book a berth for when it leaves? In other words, Success is highlighted, but have you prepared and organized your life in order to receive it? And, what IS Success to you? Money? Happiness?

This aspect indicates a need for success. It does not determine actual success, merely the need for it. This need is often opposed with the subsequent fear of failure that this might not be so, and so you may feel like you are caught in a crossfire of your own fears.

When this aspect comes up, it is an indication that many things are coming to a head. A good deal of the overall effect of the positive AND negative aspects of the 1-5-9 Trine is a sense where we eradicate the lingering guilt and inhibitions of our religious influence. It is good to be born into a religion, but bad to die in one. Let it go, then get over it, is the credo. Your Motto is: *Get on with it!*

Decimal Dice Workbook

1-6-7 Trine: *Allow Yourself the Freedom to Dream. Open up the Psychic Door to You.*

Are you finding you are flying, or breathing underwater, in your dreams? If you are, you are working well with the energy of this Trine. "Find your Freedom" is the message.

This Trine is like a mountain, implying height and majesty, yet this also indicates the laborious climb to the top. In this case the "top" has both business and spiritual aspects. We may well see you having a burning desire to achieve recognition in either (or both) of these areas when this Trine is active in your life.

This Trine augers well for spiritual and inner enlightenment, but you will need to give up a little of your personal opinions and viewpoints. The aspect often appears when you are "At Sixes and Sevens" with things in your life. It indicates you are currently needing to make an important decision, but also that you need to be prepared for the upside as well as the downside of your decision. How is your discrimination? Your Motto is: *In the Light of the Blue Dream all is a shade of Blue. What we see in the mirror is ourselves.*

1-6-8 Trine: *To Find Your Personal Truth You Must Walk through Many Storms.*

This Trine has a clear message: *Beyond your beliefs about yourself, there is the real you.* Beyond your beliefs about you and the society you live in, there is the greater reality and purpose. Beyond, far beyond, the conventions and attitudes of your personal and societal views, there is Soul. Can you Grasp the Nettle and rise above your fears so that you may look at yourself as Soul? Or will you just rebel?

Can you conquer your fears and rise above the niggling voice of your shame and regret? You may feel that you need to rebel against authority in this cycle, but the need to argue with others really comes from the loose pieces not yet in place within yourself.

Your truth will come shining like the sun. After the storms and tempests of your life, you will set yourself free.. This brings you to your motto: *The mariner is not tested in the harbour.*

The THIRD must then Appear (Paracelsus)

1-6-9 Trine: Tend the Light that Shines Within. Find A Humour in your Heart

What a curious energy this is. Here we have a drive for success and, in some cases, an equal drive for failure. At least this is how it can appear to others. At heart there is often a fear that affects our perspective on life, and if there is a degree of paranoia present as well, this loops to a self destructive tendency. You need to tend your inner garden regularly, and keep your heart clear of fears and concerns by inspecting your thoughts on a daily basis. Most of all, try to see the funny side to things… Irony is breaking out all over if we have the eyes to see this.

Remember in the first Star Wars movie when Obi-wan Knobi influences the Storm Trooper with a mental suggestion? There is a similar energy that goes with this aspect, one where you can gain a control over weaker minded persons.

There is no need for all the planning and scheduling of mind "stuff" … Relax… Let it go… Come to the council of your own heart. Your Motto is: *Appearances can be deceiving*

1-7-8 Trine: Look to see if someone is Knocking on your Door. Observe before you Act.

This is an upbeat Trine. It is an aspect that indicates things are ready to move forward in your life, especially if you are working in some area that benefits others as well as yourself. On a personal level there is often an internal paradox that you may find appealing. You may be aware that inside yourself things don't quite add up… Rather than get disaffected by this, you may well feel fascinated. It is the scientist within you that wants to see why the particular habits you may have are so curious… It may be completely inane things like: Why do you like to use a small silver spoon in soft boiled eggs, but don't like silver spoons at other times?

You may believe you are indestructible inside the walls of your own making, but you need to allow new influences in if you are to remain balanced and happy with your life. Trust that you are OK, and move forward knowing Life likes you. Your Motto is: *No man is an island.*

Decimal Dice Workbook

1-7-9 Trine: *It is only with the Heart that one sees Rightly (Look to the Intelligence of the Heart)*

This is a "big" energy. It is like the opening of Beethoven's Fifth, dramatic, strong, yet also a little strident. It certainly gets your attention, but what will you do now? There is also a slight sacrificial/religious/martyrdom thing in here where you will ruin your own best opportunities, and in this you may become fed up with yourself. But be careful not to throw out the baby with the bathwater because in order to get past your own self sabotage reflex you NEED your fear and insecurity. It's a paradox.

This is a dangerous aspect if you are somewhat unscrupulous. The energy here can lead a person into an abuse of power, friends, and put them into the mentality where they like to control and manipulate situations. This is, emotionally, a very expensive way to live.

Too often, blind impulse controls those under this influence. Think before you speak, balance the budget, don't believe what someone tells you. Cover these basics and you will be fine. Seek to rule yourself with a sense of ease, rather than a sense of "must". Your Motto is: *Never put off to tomorrow what can be done today.*

1-8-9 Trine: *Do not Cherish Opinions. Learn the Sacred Power of No Power. Find the God within.*

Where is the line between survive and thrive? We might ask ourselves, "When is enough enough?"

This is a powerful combination, though it is not necessarily a fortunate one. You may easily suffer the fate of the worldly, which is to have great wealth, yet private misfortune with bitter family disputes. This is not always the case by any means, and you may find that the negative aspects of this Trine have no effect what-so-ever in your life. It depends largely on your attitude to money and acquisition. There is an ancient truth: *If you are relaxed about the things of this world, they will be relaxed with you.*

The lesson here, curiously, is to learn the Art of NO-POWER. This means learning how to be the Catalyst rather than the Prime Mover. Your Motto is a simple one: *I do not need the approval of any God or Truth because I recognise the greater truth within.*

The THIRD must then Appear (Paracelsus)

Interpretations for Trines — **Decimal Dice Workbook**

.2-3-4 Trine: If in Doubt... Do It! Find it out!

Here we see the strong current of energy. This influence is progressive and forthright. You will find that creative solutions are always at hand for you. But the classic problem of double mindedness and double standards that plague this energy can overtake your natural flair, and this can cripple you emotionally. You need to learn and practise a "Just do it" mentality.

You may feel a conflict between a need for artistic expression and the commercial realities. Often this will never be fully settled in a person, and you may have to accept a compromise between the two. One of the main lessons involved is learned from this "creative tension" which is to get involved with a situation, but divorce yourself from the circumstances that arise as a result

Other lessons of this aspect involve more than setting goals and sticking to them, you have to set your *standards*, and stick to them. This is not ethics, but a level of expectation with the quality and value of your efforts. The Motto is: *If not this, then something better.*

2-3-5 Trine: A Shadow Lives in balanced accord with the Light. Your shadow will show you.

Do you hear in your head "Seinfeld" like questions? "Why does this person act like that?" etc. There is a bit of the Court Jester in you, however, the mind here tends to be enquiring and serious. More to the point, in this cycle you are being asked to look past the "black and white" aspects of what we call Good and Bad. In your darker moods you will find light and vice versa. You will feel a deep depression lifting very soon.

The comedian Steve Allen asked as a joke.... "What is the Speed of Dark?" Everyone laughed, but under the observation this is a serious question. What is the greater force, Dark or Light?

You can have a light, almost fragrant air about you, then flip and be dark and mysterious to others. There is often a sort of "Otherworld" appearance, and you may discover in this cycle that your are quite Psychic. Go with the Flow and see what comes of it. Your Motto is: *Challenge is necessary to Growth*

From the FIRST unto the SECOND where

Decimal Dice Workbook

2-3-6 Trine: The Mind may See Truth, but the Heart sees more clearly. Grasp the Grok (The Gestalt).

We all have heard the Beatles song "Day Tripper". Well, this can be you in a positive OR negative value.

This is a very powerful aspect, but one where you tend to get caught in your own dream. In the negative value, this indicates scheming and manipulation, and a peculiar ability to "lie the truth". This can go further, with a feeling that the world has done you wrong, but really this is usually just because you have not gotten things your way. With this aspect we learn we can get what we need through directness far better than with deception. Be upfront, be honest, and this will be a good period.

Even so, you have some very subtle traits, and few individuals will really grasp what you are about. Have you read Desiderata lately? Avoid loud and rude people as they will confuse and irritate. The words of Saint Paul are suited to your nature. In fact, they are your Motto: *It is better to understand than to be understood.*

2-3-7 Trine: Art is Subtler than Craft.

Until you clarify the energy of this Trine, you may feel like you have a cloud about you, and this can leave you feeling a little confused and out of balance. There is a great need is for direction here, but your own contrary nature can hold you in a state on indecision. Eventually, if you cannot develop a sense of purpose and direction in your life, your life may become based on this inner argument. It is a little like a Woody Allen movie, where the lead character believes that their continual inner dialogue is actually leading them somewhere... It generally does not. However, it is excellent if you want to develop traits of schizophrenia and inner separation.

Seriously, see the funny side of things, and life will work for you. You are more the artist than the craftsman. The Craftsman works on the basis of getting paid for effort by the customer, the artist works on the basis that their reward will come from divine sources.

Your Motto is from Saint Paul's comments in the Bible: *At first through the glass darkly, but then, face to face!*

The THIRD must then Appear (Paracelsus)

www.numberharmonics.org

Interpretations for Trines **Decimal Dice Workbook**

2-3-8 Trine: A Fox must be careful of chasing Chickens. Be wary of being trapped by desire.

Very Fortunate. This Aspect indicates the strong possibility of money coming to you. This may be through a gift, a lottery or by inheritance. However, there is also an adverse indication here of Loss if you are lazy and do not get out there and make things happen for yourself.

Do not rely on other people or outside assistance overmuch in this period. Financial Ability, Courage and organization are needed here... The first you can learn, preferably from a good mentor, but with courage you either have it or you have to go find it. But it takes more than Courage to win. The first rule of winning is: Clear up your personal environment. Look at what is around you. What is necessary and what is just taking up energy. Toss what you don't need.

Your Motto is: *Much Gathers More, Less Gathers Loss.*

2-3-9 Trine: The Artist has no Reason for his Love of Art, and often hates the process. Move through. It is a choice between Black and White

This is a wonderful Trine for the manifestation of things, but you must be very careful with your thoughts and your imaginings. Inside our wishes and desires are shadows and dragons that awaken as our desires are fanned.

These almost mythical creatures are real energies in the psyche and will unleash your creative force, but can you tame the wild horses? This Trine helps you tune into many different levels. It seems like a creative, manifesting force, but it is really more like uncovering what is already there. Be Warned! As you come to experience a dream or a wish come true, so too will all the associated thoughts connected with that dream wake up. The creative forces can stir up many strange energies in the ethers around you. Creativity is a process. You must survive your own process.

Diet is very important. Take care to eat only what you need in this cycle. Your Motto is: *God helps those who help themselves*

Decimal Dice Workbook

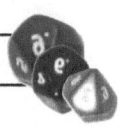

2-4-5 Trine: Grasp the Plough, Till the Earth, Enjoy the Fruit.

Even though it is a fortunate aspect, this aspect often comes up as a warning of difficulty in your life. It speaks of the Winter of Discontent, yet obviously, once you survive the Winter next comes the promise of Spring. The need for hard work and application is highlighted before the results can be enjoyed. If you have a clear sense of who and what you are, you will expect to put in the effort to gain the goal. If you have the view that life is a series of educational lessons, this Trine is most beneficial. In general, a business-like approach of accepting losses and getting on with the job is needed here.

In the negative aspect, you may experience an unrestrained and frivolous energy that weakens your resolve. Be sure to complete the task at hand and this will not be an issue for you. In the Positive aspect, you have a very generous and giving nature.

You may well have a sensitive nature, but this is no reason to not be self reliant. You need to believe in YOU. Your natural reward will come when you are ready to believe in yourself. Your Motto is: *Laugh and the world laughs with you, cry and you cry alone.*

2-4-6 Trine: Count the Cost of your Dream before you Spend It. Save your pennies, and watch them grow to more than the sum of their parts.

When we see this Trine, it tends to indicate a need to see beyond the surface of things. Are there hidden secrets in that business deal? Is a friend hiding things? What is YOUR agenda in your current tasks? Pay attention to the details in this cycle, because a jigsaw puzzle is about to fall into place. Answers will come, and the answers will often surprise.

With this Trine, you also are being told to know yourself better. If you know enough about yourself to know the difference between your true self and what is merely your trained self, this Trine will work very powerfully in your favour. If you are caught in social conditioning, this Trine will shake things up in your life, and you may find a period of change will mean new friends and travel..

Your Motto is one of sweet melancholy: *Play it again, Sam*

The THIRD must then Appear (Paracelsus)

www.numberharmonics.org

Interpretations for Trines **Decimal Dice Workbook**

2-4-7 Trine: Be Strong. Cut yourself Free.

Have you have been the Duck that didn't fly South for the Winter? Are you a leaf clinging to the vine way past Autumn. Does the ground below looks cold, and you feel dry, and all alone? When the wind of change comes you will no longer have the option of holding on. Just Let Go! Then you can enjoy the ride, or scream in terror all the way down.

As an avoidance technique you may develop a cutting and sarcastic streak. This is to keep yourself feeling secure, but all it really does is alienate you from friends. Let it go. Your own dreams are what are keeping you stuck, so let them go, and discover a whole new world awaits. So often we are attracted to what we cannot quite get, but let it all go and what is right for us will arrive..

There is always a struggle when the caterpillar must transform to the butterfly. This is part of the message of this Trine, that there will be difficulty, but that it leads to something worthwhile. Your Motto is: *The weight of the world is the world's problem, not mine.*

2-4-8 Trine: The Seed must break through its Prison of Earth to Grow

The Power of Growth is highlighted with this Aspect coming up. Yet a seed must break first through its own shell before it can sprout, and then it must break through the barrier of earth to reach the light. There is an incredible power in the first sprout. Have you ever seen how a potato shoot will push aside a large clod of earth in order to grow?

You may be offered an opportunity to grow in a stable, controlled environment. This may mean a long term job with a company, but there is also a religious connection with this Trine. In this instance, this Aspect may be connected to growing spiritually, individually, in your teaching or with your church. Surrender, letting go of the past in order to allow in the new, is what is highlighted here.

The Law of Survival states: *The person who survives best is the one who best lets thing go.* Your Motto is: *Live and let Live.*

From the FIRST unto the SECOND where

Decimal Dice Workbook

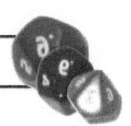

2-4-9 Trine: *I love to Rule yet I Long for Love. Do I Compromise, Forgive, or become the Tyrant?*

This is a strong aspect to call up. You need a lot of heart and a lot of courage to get through the difficult subtleties of this Trine. It is hard specifically because of its subtlety, and also because it deals with base responses, like the fight or flight response. In this case, the Fight response is Power, the Flight response is Love. You must get the two working together if you are to find happiness.

You do need to learn to work with the social courtesies in order to make things move more smoothly for you. This means compromise and the fact is a little compromise is a good thing as long as you retain the sense of your overall goal. Keep the big picture up front.

Your Motto is: *Open a door to see what new thing comes in, and then sit back and watch what goes out.*

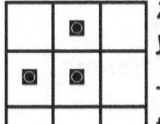

2-5-6 Trine: *Be Inspired by Life. Be Simple. Live your Life as is right for you.*

This is generally a very harmonious aspect. Considered fortunate. When this Trine comes up, you are looking to find a gain of some sort. This may be as simple as a wealth of good and useful ideas that flow, or it may mean money through inheritance of a lottery win of some sort. The doors will open and this will enhance your ability to communicate your concepts and dreams. Positions as trainers, jobs in Public Relations, and contracting out as a business adviser might be considered good avenues to follow up as far as career goes. The Trine does tend to indicate a need for decisions regarding career moves.

Yet, behind the apparent ease and simplicity of this Aspect, there is an ominous energy, a storm is brewing. Is there a skeleton in the closet? It is time to get it aired or put it to rest in a way that creates closure. Snip the loose ends, tie up the details of past associates.

Be wary of hidden secrets in contracts and false friends. Be careful with all new agreements. Your Motto is: *Yesterday is a dream and tomorrow never comes. Today is the first day of the rest of my life.*

The THIRD must then Appear (Paracelsus)

Interpretations for Trines **Decimal Dice Workbook**

2-5-7 Trine: Alone but not Lonely You are Free.

The full saying here goes: *Alone but not alone I stand in the midst of travail and destruction like a nightingale who will sing her song because the love that fills it heart comes from within. We are born alone, we will die alone, but need we be lonely in between?* The answer to all the conditions of this aspect (Both positive and negative) is surprisingly simple, and yet very difficult to put into place. It is that you need to balance out the Masculine and Feminine forces inside you. Simply listening to those you respect will help here.

Communication is the avenue for you to do this. It is indicated that you may pursue sex, specifically Tantric practices and the like, seeking this inner balance. Take care not to go overboard. It is easy to get yourself lost in a dream world of passions. It is better to be alone and free and to know yourself than be lost in a crowded room.

As you learn to enjoy your own company, you will learn to master your destiny. Your Motto is: *Only the good die young.*

2-5-8 Trine: Detachment from Fear and Circumstance leads you to Freedom.

This is an aspect of surging forces through the emotional elements of our minds and bodies. When we master the influence, we are empowered and can achieve much in this life. If we do not manage this, life will present a never ending stream of difficulties for us to solve. This is a difficult energy to master, and your health must be carefully maintained, for you may be prone to disease caused be anxiety and stress.

Listen to the whispers of the heart, not the head. This is the simple message of this Trine when it is active in your life. Your feelings will lead you more clearly than your thoughts. In this Trine you are being offered lessons that will teach you to walk in the Grace of God.

This concept of walking in Grace is a suitable image to hold for those wishing to balance the emotional side to their nature. Your Motto is: *Trust God, but Tie up your camel*

From the FIRST unto the SECOND where
www.numberharmonics.org

Decimal Dice Workbook

2-5-9 Trine: Friends are your Greatest Resource.

What is the most valuable thing in your life? Many say their money, their house, their spouse... But really, when the marriage breaks down, when the money gets spent, and when you are out on the street, your friends will take you in, feed you, and help you find another partner. Part of the energy of this Trine is asking you to look at your ability for friendship. EG: If you have made a friend of your spouse, you will never be out on the street. Simple? Few there be that realise it.

In order to find a true friend, we need to develop an attitude of service. Are you taking or giving from those in your circle? It is only in the state of selfless selfhood that we discover the subtle listening and balance that opens the door to real friendship.

Living in the moment is the great lesson here. You need to learn to appreciate and experience the simple joys of living. To this end you will find yourself drawn to country pursuits, and things that bring you closer to nature. (Even if it is shooting foxes!?) Your Motto is: *The death of the past means the growth of the future.* So, if you happen to see the burning bush... Prune It! Fight fire with hedge clippers.

2-6-7 Base Trine: Are you at 6's and 7's with yourself? True Freedom is a Mind and Heart in Balance.

This Trine can indicate turmoil and upset on the horizon unless you can find ways of pouring oil onto the troubled waters. You are generally not the Politically Correct type, however, and this may be a real effort for you. Take time to learn courtesy and patience, and you will save yourself a lot of problems in this cycle. Go that extra step, and it will all smooth out.

One of the major lessons here is the simple understanding that true freedom starts with a gentle form of honesty. There is little need to be ruthless with yourself or others, just be as honest as you can, and things will work out OK. Be careful with your natural sense of rebellion... It serves you well in breaking up old patterns, but it can also cause hidden enemies and malicious gossip that can interfere with your plans. Your Motto is: *Sufficient Unto the Day.*

The THIRD must then Appear (Paracelsus)

2-6-8 Trine: The Heart Knows. The Soul sees.

The Beatles song "Eleanor Rigby" is one you might want to pay attention to. You may well look out the window of perception to all the lonely people, yet what will you do about it? A deep compassionate energy flows through this Trine, and because of it you may feel yourself driven to act in areas that are really none of your business. The question "What to do?" has been asked for countless centuries, and you will not be answering this until you connect with your deepest aspects. You, in your case this Trine is saying "Look deeply within, and see what you can bring back to share with others"

It is not a case of doing anything for anyone, but discovering what is inside you, and sharing this when appropriate.

Look to be self employed, and focus on the small details. The level of presentation you offer will be the yardstick by which people judge you. Your Motto is one of grasping the overall truth: *There are plenty of businesses like show business!*

2-6-9 Trine: Phoenix rising. Mind your own Business. Keep Gossip from your Door

You need to keep your head for business, and your heart for the family. Try to involve family members in your business projects as much as possible, and things will move well for you. There is a great deal of intuition associated with this trine, and you need to be careful to keep things in their right compartment, mentally and emotionally. It is tricky because you have a natural feel for what others are thinking, and your natural curiosity wants to find out what it is. But stop... Let people open up and tell you rather than you dive in to find out. What happens if our curiosity takes over is that we tend to get led into other people's thoughts and ideas rather than developing our own

Your main lesson is in self sufficiency, and trusting your inner guidance. From self sufficiency a stronger trust in self and a greater connection with the Divine is realized. Your Motto is from a Tom Waites song: *The Big Print Givetth, and the Fine Print Taketh Away*

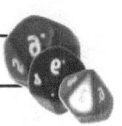

2-7-8 Trine: Listen closely to the Silence about you. Balance the Trials with Laughter.

This is a querulous and curious Trine. You may go through a period where you feel extremely uncertain about yourself and how you fit in. If you are socially conscious and of nervous disposition you may also stay a long time in studies at University, etc. This can mean maturity not arriving until your 30's. You generally need a greater self-confidence before you can express yourself clearly. Yet when the confidence arrives, all the personal inadequacy problems you have suffered will become fuel for the fire of experience.

We all know the story of how caterpillar becomes the butterfly, but the less romantic truth is that out of the cocoon there sometimes comes a moth!

Remember that Laughter is the best medicine. Humour is essential to resolve the often contrary influences of this aspect. Your Motto is: *The Sun shines equally on all, but you won't notice the sun standing in the shadows.*

2-7-9 Trine: *See through the illusion of Pleasure and Pain. Go the Extra Mile.*

This Trine can create an inherent sense of being split in two, a sort of double vision if you will. This "double" sense will continue until you begin to see through the illusion of Pleasure and Pain. The path here is all about balance, and removing the poison of toxic elements such as fear and gossip from the orbit of your thoughts. It may mean Travel, or leaving your place of work.

Part of the life lesson from this Trine is to resolve the various Paradoxes. IE: Pain and Pleasure, High and Low, Rich and Poor, etc. Of course, there is no paradox. The Law states: **Present circumstances are earned by the individual as a result of Karma**. If this aspect has come up for you, it may be suggesting that you take a more "Cold Fish" approach to things. Learn to be detached.

The words to remember here are also your Motto: *If everyone swept their own doorsteps, we would all have a clean street.*

The THIRD must then Appear (Paracelsus)

Interpretations for Trines **Decimal Dice Workbook**

2-8-9 Trine: Arrival means Acceptance. Leaving the Past behind and Giving Yourself a break.

A curious aspect. Watch negative thoughts or gossip, because they may return one day to haunt you. When you feel depressed or deflated, the negative aspects of your life can seem much larger than they really are, and because of this is SEEMS difficult. Try to apply logic and rational thinking to events, rather than emotional responses, and you will do better both financially and emotionally. You are bigger than your problems.

"We are all in it together" should be the words at the forefront of your thoughts. This understanding will give you a great ability to appreciate the problems and issues of your neighbours, and so you will be better placed to negotiate a path to resolution.

Be wary of ambitious people. Be especially wary if they want to pull you into their orbit and get you to support their cause. Your Motto is: *Learn to see the wood for the trees.*

3-4-5 Trine: The Fountain Is ready to Burst Forth. Initiation by Fire or Water.

Spiritually, the aspects of Fire and Water are what create the breath of life. In this respect you have to meld your internal opposites and create a new "you".

The energy of this aspect will drive you (if you let it) past personal insecurity into a clear communication your work or principles. This can make you very successful. In particular, this Trine is good for manifesting CREATIVE Ventures. Even if you find out that what you have to offer has little value to anyone outside your immediate circle, it will still be of use in this regard. Write that book, paint, dance!

The better part of our problems will tend to come from other people's projections and shadows. If you can understand this, you can solve a lot of personal issues at this time. Think Judo, turn it to your advantage. If you can deal with this, you will do well in this cycle.

Your Motto is: *You can lead a horse to water, but you can't make it drink.* (But it could as easily be the Nike Motto "Just do it!")

Decimal Dice Workbook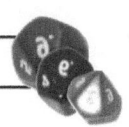

3-4-6 Trine: Truth needs a Peg upon which to Hang. *A foot in Heaven and a foot of the ground works only if you are prepared to stand still.*

There is a progressive possibility when this Trine comes up, yet remember that all of the energy here can be completely reversed, and you may end up a confused old man, wandering about not knowing where to hang their hat. This is why you need to be careful about developing trustworthy friendships. In case you go off the rails, you will need someone to point you in the right direction once more.

Angular and precise, you do not muck about with those you see as being no-hopers. You are generally are good at defining goals and organizing your personal life so that these can be achieved.

The greatest fruit of your endeavours tends to appear later in your life, but if you keep a smile on the face, your youth will be a serviceable experience. Your Motto is: *Love and liberty for all* … But if you are at liberty to choose to either serve or rule, you prefer to rule.

3-4-7 Trine: Trim the Hedge. Over the Wall and past your barriers lies Yourself.

This tends to be a thick and rather unpleasant Trine, with a constant "push pull" energy about it, but if you can look inside your problems or your sense of depression at this point you will actually find a huge inspiration. When you come to understand that the apparently "negative" effect is the pressure of your inner doors opening to a whole new wave, you will jump the hurdles inside yourself and find a tremendous freedom.

You would like to be generous, but the stoic side of your nature will generally prefer to serve itself. It is not quite being selfish, but being self reliant. You may find problems when you expect others to do the same. Beware the "Small" petty nature or others and yourself. In this cycle you can move past the small world of Self by getting out and enjoying the world. Only then will the energy of this Trine starts working in your favour. Your may 'think' your motto is : "*I think therefore I am*" but really, "*I sink, therefore I swim.*"

The THIRD must then Appear (Paracelsus)

Interpretations for Trines **Decimal Dice Workbook**

3-4-8 Trine: Believe in your Right to Live. Cherish Life. Believe in yourself and you will grow.

This can be a very Karmic aspect. It is often the classic Trine for the unsung hero. Have you been carrying the burden with little help? This Trine is saying it is all about to change, but when? The poverty struck artist and lonely housewife suddenly find a new horizon, which fills them with hope and vigour, but when do we actually get to the horizon?

You must develop a "carry on regardless" attitude if you are to open the door to success here. If you manage to click in on this attitude, you will unleash the power of creativity in every aspect of your life. If we work with the sometimes disturbing energy present here, and learn to master it, life will come into clear focus... Only then do we understand the purpose we are here for.

Your Motto is: *Sandcastles may fall down with the tide, but what a joy to build more.*

3-4-9 Trine: *Moving with the Current, Flowing with the Tide, You Discover your Path.*

The Law of Non-resistance rules this aspect. Go with the flow, and see what comes of things.

It is a noble, resonant Trine, one that encourages the person affected to stay focussed on the end goal. This, though many will say otherwise, is the easiest way to succeed in life. The details will come, of course, but if we keep the overview uppermost in our minds details will remain as details to us, and not bog us down into "obstacle thinking". Think like the hunter, allow your goal to come to you. Position yourself well and reduce your effort.

This Trine indicates a great down pouring of energy but you will need a practical nature to contain this. If you are practical and balanced in your physical world, you will find success. Paradoxically, the Silent, Focussed Pursuit of the objective is the precursor to true surrender, and counts towards the true practice of non-resistance. Your Motto is: *Resist not evil, but don't invite it in for dinner.*

Decimal Dice Workbook

3-5-6 Trine: I can Create, given the Will. Yet, What is My Will?

This is the artists Trine. Are you ready to go buy the easel and paint? Seriously, your expression of "art" can occur in numerous ways, and not necessarily in painting. In your present life, look to add that extra flair in what you do, add your little bit of art to things. When you do, money people will be attracted to you. It's a curse and a blessing. We must learn how best to communicate our needs to these folk, and THEN the lesson of how to deal with the money consciousness begins. In particular the lesson is in how not to be abused and confused by the worldly power that inevitably comes with the "money" people.

There may be Fame indicated here, and this can be either famous or infamous. It may simply be a fleeting recognition or a lifetime achievement award. Who knows! But something is on its way as we speak. Your motto comes from the famous words of Guru Adrian: *Half the Fun is Having Fun.*

3-5-7 Trine: Compassionate Service brings the Buddha into Your Heart. Seeds planted will grow

The Positive Aspects here are very healthy, yet the negative ones are extremely unhealthy. Your positives are enthusiasm, a happiness that can shine, and a genuine love for people and for life. The negative can be a deep depression. You may feel out of place in your family and your work, and this can start a whole chain of negative effects. Trust is the lesson. Trust your instincts, and THEN take care that you leave the gate to your heart shut to all but those you trust.

Perception is a strong point with you, so look for a field of endeavour where your natural perceptive abilities can be used. This is a good aspect for the healer, or those who choose to work in a field where they touch and help people. This Trine is also good for those who seek to understand the inner motivations of the human race.

The Motto here is: *Hold a kind heart and a clear head…. United with myself I stand strong.*

Interpretations for Trines   **Decimal Dice Workbook**

3-5-8 Trine: Who Understands the Poets?

This Trine can be quite tricky. You have a poet inside you that even you won't necessarily understand. You may find yourself drawn to causes, and the doing of a thousand things that other people will say is insane, a waste of time, and proof that you are crazy... But something inside you compels you to act.

Emotional impact is the desired goal with you, and very often you will achieve just this. A career on the stage or a position where you can unleash your emotional energies may be an ideal path for you. Maybe join a local Repertory Theatre company?

Focus will bring you both clarity and freedom. The best way to achieve this Focus is to practice doing one thing at a time. It is the "One Step at a Time" attitude that will clear the mind and emotions of clutter, allowing you to get on with the things at hand. Who understands the Poets? Give it time, and 'you' will. When you do, your vision will be splendid.

Your Motto is: *Let go of the Angst, feel each fresh, new day*

3-5-9 Trine: A Heart Married to a Purpose is Free.

If you are going to find a degree of happiness you will need to develop a contemplative approach to life. This is not a passive state, but a deeply considered approach that thinks before acting. What you need to understand here is the Ancient Principle of the Three Moons.

This Principle is simply the practice of patience when you do not understand a situation of a thing. Slowly understanding grows, like the moon growing from the new moon to the full moon. When the light is clear and you can see what is in front of you, you know the way to go in any given situation. This brings Right Action.

The principle is: Act only when you feel you have understood the situation. Take your time to grasp what is before you, and act accordingly. Your motto is: *The mill wheels of the Gods grind slowly, but exceedingly fine. (*You want to be the baker or the bread?)

From the FIRST unto the SECOND where

www.numberharmonics.org

Decimal Dice Workbook

3-6-7 Trine: *The Wolf is happiest with a Family.*

This is an interesting energy you have picked up here. Alone but not lonely, you can find a solitary joy in reading a book, washing the dog, and generally being disconnected from other people for lengths of time. Of course, the Wolf generally has a family to go home to, and the combination of wandering free then coming back home is ideal for you. Difficult to attain, but ideal.

A warning! There is the danger of falling into the Perfection Trap here, and while we must seek to do the best we can, we must also learn that enough is enough. Inside you there is often an agitating influence. This "agent provocateur" is always seeking a new way of doing something, a new method to make things better.

There are two things at work against you... 1/ A lack of inner confidence, and 2/ poor timing. The clue to working it out is that your personal timing is tied to your level of self worth. This is a tricky Aspect, one that requires hard work. Focus on developing a secure home life, and things will work better for you. Your Motto is: *My level of consciousness is my level of acceptance.*

3-6-8 Trine: *Harebrained Scheme or Brilliant Work? Time will decide ...*

Those affected by this Trine have a tendency to live in a world of theory and unreality. Insanity is only a hairsbreadth from genius, and you may well find that under the influence of this Trine that you walk the fine line between both. This can be fun or frustrating, depending on the degree of flexibility you have. The Rule here is: Emotional *Rigidity is the enemy of fun*. Rigor Mortis is best left to dead people.

A major lesson here is to learn how best to live in this world. This generally means learning practicality, which means moving out from the world of theory. Get more in tune with those around you and your feeling and you will do well. Be wary of separation on a personal level from loved ones. The sense of disconnection fades when we start having FUN. Your Motto is: *Truth Never Varies*.

The THIRD must then Appear (Paracelsus)

Interpretations for Trines **Decimal Dice Workbook**

3-6-9 Trine: The Mind is your enemy until it is your friend: Know what you want, then let it go.

The energy of this Trine can be like a Laser. It can cut through steel, heal the wounded or (as we read in the Science Fiction books) destroy worlds. You mind can be a weapon of mass destruction or the tool that heals... That is, if you have yourself together. Otherwise it is a weapon of mess and distraction. Focus on keeping your world in order, and things will go better for you.

One of the negative aspects of this line is the use of hypnotic "commands". This can be as subtle as the woman using a flick of an eyelash to gain control over a man, or as blatant as the propaganda events in Nazi Germany, but whatever the extent of the pattern, the goal is the search for personal power. The positive aspect is a powerful internal learning process. In this you have the potential to recognise your role in life, and as a result find great contentment. Your Motto needs to be: *If not this, then something better.*

3-7-8 Trine: What's it to Be? God or Mammon?

This aspect is saying that you have to be careful with your choices at this point in time. What are you wishing for in your heart of hearts? More to the point, will the desire for this become the basis on how you will conduct your life? We all have a need for love, wealth and happiness, but what "is" wealth and love and happiness to you?

The wealth you seek may be a deeper understanding of yourself and the inner workings of life, but generally most people do not run this deep, and your choices will be more towards the right partner, the right house, etc

Most will select the low road, and the pursuit of Mammon. This means their life will be one of Karma. You can choose differently at any time, however, and this will alter the entire framework of your thinking. Your Motto is: *I give back to life what I can in this moment. As I have received so I give.*

From the FIRST unto the SECOND where

www.numberharmonics.org

Decimal Dice Workbook

3-7-9 Trine: *A Secure Foundation builds a Secure House.* **Stone on Stone, Milarepa built 7 times.**

We know the saying "Go the extra mile" ... Well, if you organize things well right from the start, going that extra inch in the beginning and making sure the foundations are good will mean you will save yourself running many miles later on. This applies to relationships, employment, in fact everything in your life. Luck is what happens after you have planned everything properly. This is the energy of this Trine. It attracts good luck IF you plan properly and secure yourself against adversity.

The Tibetan Saint, Milarepa, had to build the house 7 times for the Master Marpa. Why? Because he was full of the poisons of passion. The lesson here is to be able to carry on alone if needs be. Patience is the essential element for those with this Trine affecting their chart.

Your Motto is: "A man who knows he is right forms a majority of one against the crowd." Thoreau

3-8-9 Take care... *Your Altruism can Cost you! Thinking too much, doing to little is expensive. Allow your Ambition. Allow you Humour.*

A creative carelessness can run with the energy of this aspect. It is a wonderful thing and is quite childlike, and yet underneath there may be darker clouds brewing. The energy of Past Time can surface with this Trine, and it may be that reading a book on Egypt you fall into the imagination of how it was... And then you find yourself tuning in to all things Egyptian. This opens psychic doors to that time, and that energy can flow in to your present experience in odd ways.

This Trine does indicate a sort of mental short circuit. Mostly the "short circuit" occurs in your transition from the altruistic youth to the world weary wise man. Get the message? You can find wisdom, but hang onto the youthful aspects of joy. Watch out for the Short Circuit and the fraying of temper. Your Motto is: *People do what they do because they believe their actions are what is best for their survival.*

The THIRD must then Appear (Paracelsus)

www.numberharmonics.org

Interpretations for Trines   **Decimal Dice Workbook**

4-5-6 Trine: Ambition knows no Boundaries

This is a curious and sometimes very powerful Trine. It crosses many boundaries. You may find that business is suddenly becoming a focus of activity, or it may be that your home life has large, red flags waving. Something somewhere needs attention. You have an intuition as to what it is, but you need to focus and sort something out ... Bring out the hard nose business practicality side of yourself, and get it sorted.

This Trine indicates the Will to Persevere. In this next cycle you also have the potential of developing a strong sense of your own worth.

In the negative this aspect can be very destructive. You may be carrying a great anger which is often disguised as self righteousness. In the positive great progress spiritually and materially can be made.

The major lesson here is to loosen up your social inhibitions, with a goal to become more spiritually free rather than practice the libertine ways. Your Motto is: *When the student is ready the Master appears.*

4-5-7 Trine: There is a Freedom in the Darkness; Understand that Few will Understand You.

This can be a difficult and sombre vibration to work through. It may require a great deal of perseverance before any successful outcome appears. However, as you work through the sense of mental complication that often arises here, things will go easier. Indeed, the aspect becomes very LUCKY. The trick here is in keeping focussed on your ambition and your goal, yet also relaxing and enjoying your moments as they come and go. It is a difficult balancing act as your mind will often want to interfere with this process.

This Trine won't give you class and style, but if you do have it, you can really work it to considerable advantage with this energy in your life. Lateral Thinking works well for you. In this will gain you a good understanding of the human condition. There is an intriguing, hidden side to you. You like the shadows and the dark places of the mind. Your Motto: *It is better to understand than to be understood.*

From the FIRST unto the SECOND where
www.numberharmonics.org

Decimal Dice Workbook

4-5-8 Trine: Are You a Soul with a Body, or a Body with a Soul? You will become the song that you sing.

There is a dark and mysterious aspect to this Trine, but you may not see it unless you are put into some strange and exotic situation. It may be that you are caught up in some powerfully dramatic event, and only in these circumstances does this "hidden" energy come forward. In any case, under pressure you can perform well and as a curious aspect to this, you may push yourself to limits looking for the "Buzz" that kicks in the deep survival instinct in you.

If you are of a higher mind and not needing so much in the way of material goods, this aspect is good. It is more than good, it is a ticket to the Higher Worlds. However, if you are materially minded with their goals and aspirations, periods of bad luck may well seem to dog your every move. Even so, there is good luck as well.

The Pythagoreans said, "To become what we sing, this is the price the Gods exact for song." Your Motto is: *The price of freedom is eternal vigilance.*

4-5-9 Trine: Intention, not Hope, is the faith that moves Mountains. What do you Intend?

Though the winds may blow, the steadfast man is strong and certain in his truth because of his Faith. Faith of itself is an attitude that is little understood. It is not a fragile wishing, nor a wilful push, but a sincere expectation. True Faith is more than an attitude, it is a knowing and experience combined. It is a deep sense of gestalt that has come to rest in the heart through the tests of time and tide. How do we pass from the impermanent dreams (with all their assorted baggage of fear and uncertainty) into the simple reality of Faith? In a word, INTENTION. Within the world of our intentions the first blocks of a true faith are placed. Intention, not hope, is the cornerstone of our deepest truth.

When you are in YOUR truth? Do you have a quiet determination that is impossible to stop? Are you chaff in the wind or Wheat?. Your motto is (as a result): *Quo Usque Tandem *How Long Still?"*

The THIRD must then Appear (Paracelsus)

4-6-7 Trine: From Darkness to Light, from one to the many to the one ... The Cycle Turns until you grasp who and what you are.

Are you feeling at Sixes and Seven's? This Trine will help ground you. However, this is a fairly full on, in your face, get out of my way the train is coming through vibe here. This is the type of energy that prefers to break down barriers rather than jump over or go around them. How will you do this? It's not so much an army but the coordination of natural forces that will shake the resistance until it become malleable.

Is there a divine right of Kings? Others will not necessary respect your vision of things. Expect difficulty and you won't be disappointed

You have a Major Life Lesson with this Trine. It is simply called "the Secret of Life". Are you ready for this? I will give it to you, and you can maybe use it as your Motto as well: *One plus One equals Two.*

4-6-8 Trine: Freedom is found in the Little Things. Keep a record of your thoughts.

This is a Money Trine, so called because the individual with this aspect is very likely to make a lot of money in their lives. If it is not actual cash, it will be a wealth of some sort, perhaps even a spiritual wealth of wisdom and knowledge. This of course is the greatest of the riches we can earn... for this we can take with us past the grave.

Many people with this aspect highlighted do very well for themselves, not just with money, but on many levels. It is a Trine of Independence, so learn to think for yourself and you will be OK.

You will do best in self employment, either in your own business or in contractual arrangements. You will need to be independent in some way, both at work and in relationships. But HOW independent>? You are the type that is happy to sail your boat into uncharted waters, but believe me it helps to leave a message that says where you are going. In this regard, it's important to keep a diary of your dreams and thoughts. Your Motto is: *If not me, then who?*

Decimal Dice Workbook

4-6-9 Trine: Whom do you Serve? Are you making God in Your Image?

There are more people who serve no God, no purpose, than those who do we would generally imagine. But this is not really true. People worship many things. It may be the Pop Star, the rich food, a football team that you worship. When you place anything above your natural meeting with each moment as it comes, you are making God in your Image. In other words, you are creating something to be more important than the truth of yourself in this moment.

You are SOUL. Soul is Eternal, Soul lives in the Moment, Soul knows only the highest path of Truth and Love. Until you resonate with the truth of this, you will be beating a hollow drum. Until you connect with this, you will not connect to the Circle of Life within yourself. Your Motto would do well being: *In God we Trust ...* Which brings up the question... What God do you serve?

4-7-8 Trine: The Herald of Karma. Your fate is determined by the Quality of Your Heart.

Osiris weighs your heart against a feather... How free are you? How PURE are you? Any heaviness will send you to the underground, but if you have lightness and good will in your heart you will rise up to the Tuat and take your place beside the Gods. Socrates was forced to take the Hemlock because he suggested that by lifting the heart into the Spiritual Currents, we could rise up unto the spiritual ether and as ourselves become as a God. Who can say what the truth is? Consider this fact: When you stand in final judgement of your worth, when your heart is weighed, will anyone be looking at your university degree?

Despite the apparent heaviness this Trine is saying "create and dream" . You will make a good inventor or innovator. If you are focussed on Art, you will want to be the best artist. If your interest is in fashion, you will dream of Paris catwalks and supermodels. There is no half way point in your imagination of where you want to go... Just find the highest peak and start climbing. Expect some scratches.

Your motto is: *Why climb the mountain? Because it is there.*

The THIRD must then Appear (Paracelsus)

www.numberharmonics.org

Interpretations for Trines — Decimal Dice Workbook

4-7-9 Trine: Climb the Sacred Stair. A Door Opens. To Touch Love is to Breath the Atoms of Life ... It is a perfume or a stench by your attitude

This is an interesting aspect, combining a physical tenacity with a Silent Spiritual Strength. In a number of cases we will see this evidence itself as actual physical prowess, and we find a robustness of spirit with this Trine. There is a CAN DO energy to here that is refreshing, but if you get hooked up into emotional conflicts you become worthless to yourself and others.

You may like the idea of joining movements, especially humanitarian causes, but what is driving you? Love or Hate? You are being asked to look at the "polarity" of emotion inside yourself. If you have an interest in success (and some don't here) you need to understand and practice the Law of Silence. This is more knowing what to say, rather than not saying anything. In this respect, you will develop an ability to observe without buying emotionally or mentally into the process before you. Your Motto is: *Always go that extra inch, especially when you want to give up. Go the extra inch.*

4-8-9 Trine: Silence before the Howling Gale. Fold the Sails and wait till it is passed.

This is a time to hold fast. Batten down the things that can be shaken in the storm, and bring in the food and fuel you will need. This is not a long Winter of Discontent that comes, but a sharp and often sudden fury that blows itself out fairly quickly. Life may be tempestuous in the cycles that unfold in your life at this point, but you will learn to ride the storm. Indeed, in time you will come to understand that this is the best part. The sailor in port will enjoy the time with friends and family, but the heart of the mariner is always calling for the ocean.

You may have a need to break away from convention, and if so you should arm yourself with a dry wit and a sharp sword of cynicism, as well as many pointed observation to comment on. Thin Seinfeld.

The lesson is to see beyond the illusion of pleasure and pain, and thus begin the journey into the depths of your beingness. Your Motto is an odd one: *I laugh because the tears are too hard to stop.*

From the FIRST unto the SECOND where

www.numberharmonics.org

Decimal Dice Workbook

5-6-7 Trine: Humanity is You ... So helping yourself get happy will help everyone around you.

There is a natural helpful nature that goes along with the energy of this Trine, and yet also a driving force that wants to make things happen NOW. What happens is that you may get polarized between your happy helpful self, and the one who wants to make it happen. This can leave you feeling "At sixes and seven's" and your solution may well be to talk about it! This is a Trine suited to the counsellor or person in a listening role, because you will find that helping other, especially by listening, will make your own issues fade away.

Whatever your profession, there is usually a period of introspection and difficulty faced by people with this Trine. The journey is to discover yourself. The surprise is, in doing so you come to understand every person.

Acceptance of Self is a big lesson here. Acceptance frees the heart and mind, and allows contentment to grow on what would otherwise be rocky soil. Your motto is: *Get past the past*.

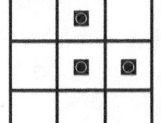

5-6-8 Trine: A Curse can appear as a Blessing, and Vice-Versa. Be careful of False Friends.

This is generally a fortunate aspect for finance. You may find you are dealing with others people's money at first, but this will changes as you move into and understand the Money Consciousness. Experience and time will bring about an accumulation of life's necessities and luxuries. When you possess this aspect you must be careful of the temptation to do things too quickly. Stability comes through slow growth as a rule, though there are exceptions. The way it often works is that you may be working for years with little seeming progress, and then suddenly all falls into place.

In reality the growth had been happening over a long period of time, but of course the roots that grow the tree cannot be seen. When the right season arrives, you will bloom.

The Law you need to work with is the Law of Attitude. Your Motto is: *As the Winter speaks of the spring, the spring speaks of the winter.*

The THIRD must then Appear (Paracelsus)

5-6-9 Trine: Limitations and Obstacles are Life's Ladders. Snakes or Ladders are a roll of the Dice

You may be faced with issues relating to both business and the home. To work through this, you need to look at the inner spiritual aspect of these as well as the mundane. How did you come to be in this situation? What brought you here? You are receiving the gifts of heaven, and this Trine can represent a highly inspirational period, but will you see through the fog? You have a chance to get above the morass of the Social Consciousness but many will try and pull back the Soul who dares leave the Gossip Circle. You have a choice, stay with the past, or move onto something new.

To do this properly, you will need to figure out your needs, and the first step is to realise the difference between your needs and wants. A clue: Needs are things less vulnerable to change. (Shelter, food, etc.) Your Motto is: We do not choose the frame of our destiny, but we certainly can choose what picture we hang in the frame.

5-7-8 Trine: Be Open ... Accept that Life Loves You ... but be prepared for the storm.

Some combinations have an odd vibration that is both lucky and yet unlucky. The pivotal point between good and bad luck in this instance is COMMUNICATION. Really, luck is an energy that is simply a possibility. If you are communicating you can convert these possibilities into something that works to your advantage. EG: An Insurance salesman was training a new recruit. The problem was that the potential buyer took one look at the fellow and said "GETOUT!" The man immediately turned to his recruit and shouts at him... "You heard the man, GET OUT!" Then he sat down and sold the fellow a policy

Learning to get your energy out is important. When you stop complaining and start doing something useful in life, all the energy expands outwards. It is like turning the key in the lock, the doors start to open and you feel really good about yourself and life in general. Your Motto is: *If the mud sticks, wash it off. If there is smoke, stop hanging around smokers.*

From the FIRST unto the SECOND where
www.numberharmonics.org

Decimal Dice Workbook

5-7-9 Trine: Where is the difference between your WANT and your NEED? Are you listening to Aspirations or Whispers?

Every day, we choose from two jars at the portal of our being... the Jar of Aspiration, or the Jar of Whispers. Which will you choose? Aspiration leads you to pursue your highest ideals and is focussed on making this day better than the one before. Listening to your whispers leads you into the shadow self, and all the doubts and fears you secretly hold. This Trine is saying you are now at a point where you can become more aware of the secret processes hidden in your mind.

You will awaken to a choice in this cycle... Continue with the social games, or become more honest and direct. Have you the courage to face your Shadow? Are you willing to accept that your humanity is both darkness and light? Saint Paul said: *"At first through the Glass Darkly, but then, Face to Face!"* When you understand this, you have solved the riddle of this Trine. Your Motto is: *If it's not broke, don't fix it!*

5-8-9 Trine: If Wishes were Horses, Beggars would Ride. There is little Joy in an Ivory Tower.

This is an altruistic combination which we see often in people in government and university positions. Those with the Trine active in their life can carry a certain aloofness. This Ivory Tower syndrome annoys "mere mortals" but what is worse is the arrogant person who has achieved nothing, yet imagines that they are important and influential.

On the positive aspect, you can be enthusiastic and responsive to other peoples ideas, not just your own. However, good intentions are not enough, and Murphy's Law applies... If it can go wrong, it probably will. Remember, Murphy was an optimist!

This Trine is under the Law of Completion ... Do what you have agreed to do. Don't start what you won't finish, but if you are in the midst of something you cannot complete, write down all you have done and the reason why you cannot finish the task, and resign. You have to keep your confidence up. The motto here is: *Seize the Day*

The THIRD must then Appear (Paracelsus)

www.numberharmonics.org

Interpretations for Trines

6-7-8 Trine: Patience is Needed.

Do you feel you have been living at sixes and sevens with life and the situations and circumstances around you? This Trine is telling you it is time to finish this cycle. You will need patience and a good deal of application, but focus on what the problems are, and one by one remove them from your life.

In this cycle, elimination is better than negotiation. If you haven't used it in 6 months, throw it out. Do you have a project? Get to it quickly... Don't wait about, just get to it BUT you will need patience because "it" will take time to work itself out. Take care with the way you approach things in this cycle. This Trine often appears at a pivotal point in your life, so make haste slowly.

Are you suffering setbacks from unknown sources? The answer may be simple. A solution here is often with *Credentials ! Find a way for others to believe in you.* This can be by way of a track record, a university degree or simply a body of respect from your peers. When you get your credentials everything will move more easily for you. Your Motto: *God helps those who help themselves.*

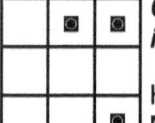

6-7-9 Trine: Are you at Odds with your Mind? Look into your Heart and find the Solution.

Have you been feeling at "Sixes and Sevens" lately? Maybe this is because you are thinking too much, and feel a little isolated. This aspect is saying: Slow down, take it easy, relax, make friends. Which is easy if you know how, but if you knew how you wouldn't have to be told to slow down, take it easy, etc. Put on the emotional and mental brakes, and rest.

You need to learn the Law of Silence. This is not found in being completely silent, rather it is in knowing what to say in any given situation. We all have ideals but we can only practice these only we have a deep confidence and self-knowledge about ourselves. It's all here waiting for you. The gift is already here, can you find it?

There is a message that you may need a mentor if you are to make the best progress in this cycle. Your Motto: *Not my will, but thine Oh Lord.* (as well as: *If not this, then something better ...*)

Decimal Dice Workbook

6-8-9 Trine: A Moment with the Divine Rests between the Hurdles.

There is a curious "end of cycle" energy at work here. A whole load of "Stuff" is about to end, which may be good or bad, depending on your circumstances. Usually, though, the indication is for the finish of a negative cycle, and this tends to mean moving on to something better.

Primarily, in this period you are being told to be sure to protect your boundaries, and in particular to be careful about taking on the energies of others in this cycle. If you do not protect the fences and keep the gate shut, you may be letting n energies that will set off a whole new round of drama.

This is a noble Trine, one that has high ideals and best intentions. But you know what they say about the road to hell, and good intentions. Drop the White Knight from the repertoire of social habits.

We are dealing with Fear of Failure and some very basic instinctual energies with this pattern. Take your time and move thoughtfully and carefully through this next cycle. Don't rush things. Your Motto is: *Do unto other as you would have them do unto you…*

7-8-9 Trine: Your Journey to Life begins. Give to Life and Life returns the gift.

Let go of the Strings that Bind. Life is for Living. It's a gift and so ask: How can I return the Gift? How can you free yourself of your past conditioning and move into the greater vision of yourself as Soul? Your job when this Powerhouse Trine comes up is to solve this very question.

Many with this aspect coming up feel idealistic and altruistic, but we are really learning to be practical. When this Trine is being called, it is saying "Give to Life in a practical way." Even so, you are being called to reach for a broader vision. Look for a better job, or a more USEFUL position. Your life is about to move into new and fertile directions. But have you planted the seeds for the coming season?

Fact is, most people are so enmeshed in the strings and ownership tags of everyone, they really don't know what direction to go in. Vines entangle, weeds choke. Clear them out of your life. Look inwardly for the answers, and follow what comes from your divine guidance. The Motto here is: *As Spirit Moves me*

The THIRD must then Appear (Paracelsus)

Closing Notes on the Pythagorean Trines

Little has been written about the Pythagorean Trines since the 18th Century. There are many reasons for this, but the major one is a curious tale of literary misdirection and plagiarism.

It all started in the modern era with a book published in 1903 "Mysteries of Sound and Number" that claimed to be "True Pythagorean Numerology". In the book many interesting things were introduced, but in truth, this was not really a core truth, but a mishmash of many concepts, most of which revolved around using numbers to win at horse racing.

However, this became "the" reference book for many of the writers up till Cheiro published his "Book of Numbers" in the 1930's. This was a book that spoke of the Chaldean tradition. Well, as it turned out Cheiro's book was far closer to true Pythagorean Numerology than the so-called original "source book". (Granted that Pythagoras studied and used many Chaldean Principles in his own work. They were contemporaneous systems.)

In time, both of these main sources were mingled together, and in the process very few authors ever credited their source. (The usual practice for the time, I might add). What happened was a literary "Chinese Whisper". Books derived from the first scrolls became "the" reference books for the next batch of Numerology writers, and so on. The source information was largely lost.

Worse, people then starting inventing their own systems. Some, like Goodwin's, are very good. Most "systems", however, are regurgitated nonsense.

In all it got pretty muddled as to what Pythagorean, Chaldean or Kabala (Judaic Numerology - called Gematria by the Masons) actually was. Worst of all, the most BASIC PRINCIPLE of Pythagorean thought was, for the greater part, missed altogether. This is simply; the Law of Three.

The Law of Three states: Where there is One, it calls unto a Second, whereupon the Third shall appear. **Paracelsus** re-phrased this in the 15th Century to "From the First unto the Second, from whence the Third must appear"

Our simple proof of the importance of the TRINE, or the structure of THREE is that a great deal of Pythagorean Mathematics was resolved from a study of harmonics and music. The most basic principle of Music is the CHORD, or the combination of 3 (or more) notes.

There is no Pythagorean Principle that is devoid of the concept of the Trine. Trigonometry, Surveying, all these essential mathematics the Pythagoreans evolved incorporated the notion of the THIRD in everything. And so in seeking to be true to the Pythagorean Legacy we give you this study.

This Combination of THREE NUMBERS is what we call a TRINE, and this brings us to the heart of the most basic of the Pythagorean Principles. I trust you will enjoy playing with the concepts presented here.

Decimal Dice Workbook

The Rules for Understanding Trines

1. Always ask a Question before throwing the Dice
2. Then: Be prepared for the Question to Change
3. Then: Be prepared for the Answer to be something that you will not necessarily like
4. Understand that the process you are entering into is one that encourages CHANGE. Expect change and you will never be disappointed
5. Allow yourself to contemplate what a Trine says. Give it time before deciding on what it means to you. Or at least give yourself room to alter your understanding. Why? So often, as one "click" of understanding happens it changes the nature of how you read everything that came before.
6. Never throw the Dice on behalf of another without their permission (Unless you are the guardian or parent of the person in question)
7. Try not to interpret for another what a particular Trine might mean. Rather, seek to give the person room to find what "they" feel it might mean.
8. Always look at the opposite of what a particular Trine might be saying, and see how this fits. Often we find a Trine will get reversed in its meaning.
9. Be nice to animals and pay the bills as best you can. If you can't pay the bills, be nicer to animals.

VARIATIONS: *There are many variations you can incorporate into your "Trine Finding" with the Dice. One simple example is to throw the 10 sided Die TWICE, then add up the two to get the third. IE: You throw a 6 than a 8, this adds to 14. "Add Down" the 14 to 5 ... Now rearrange the numbers from LOWEST to HIGHEST. (5 / 6 / 8) Look up the 5-6-8 Trine and see how it relates to your question.*

It is as simple as this! Play with the Dice, and they will become playful

The THIRD must then Appear (Paracelsus)

There is a PATTERN to Everything

You will have already come to recognize that there is a PATTERN behind everything we do with these random throws of the Dice. Now we are going to discover how various aspects you already are familiar with can be combined with things like DATES (Birth Date, etc.) to create new and surprising Interpretations.

All we have studied is derived from the Study of Number. (See: Book of Number series, same author) In simple terms, everything has been tested and researched. We have used the Pythagorean Techniques for over 30 years and have done thousands of charts. The percentage of replies to the effect that the character profiles, with the subsequent interpretations and predictions, seemed miraculous in their accuracy is close to 90%. But HOW can NUMBERS show so much? How so much accurate information could be derived from Dates and Names.

It is really just the following of a pattern. A date is a series of cycles, and though it seems haphazard, life moves mathematically. Despite the apparent randomness of events, one thing "does" lead to another, and by correctly analyzing what the FIRST thing is, we can determine the "likely" steps that follow from that point.

Life is not a closed book. Everything is open to change, but when change comes, it too will follow certain "rules" or parameters. And what is more, the "Change" of itself is part of the potential that was set into motion with the first step.

The sum of this is very simple: We cannot determine the frame of our Destiny, but we CAN determine what picture we will hang in it. The Dice will teach you about the FRAME, or what is generally called the archetype, you are currently inside. What you DO with it is what counts. This is a matter of choice. And here is the truth: We CHOOSE our path by choosing to understand, or ignore, the present.

Making the "right" choice, however, that's the part no one can teach you. Therefore: We wish you clarity with your choices.

BOOK THREE: Decimal Dice Series

Advanced Games Workbook
Looking at highly skilled Divination Games

INDEX:	
Simple Addition	Page 99
The Matrix Map	Page 100
Explanation of the Matrix Pattern	Page 105
Finding the Trine in the Matrix	Page 108
Matrix Studies	
Finding Doublets in the Matrix	Page 111
Advanced Matrix Studies	Page 116
The Present, Past, Future Game	Page 127
References and URL's	Page 142

Iacta Alea Est: *This is the famous quote from Julius Caesar which he shouted to his troops as he made to cross the Rubicon. This action is what led to him become the Dictator of Rome, and brought the name of Julius Caesar forever into the History Books*

For many years this quote has been translated as "The Die is Cast" meaning that blind fate has already decided the outcome of this venture. However, some disagree and suggest that the true translation would be "Let the Dice Fly High". Meaning, "I am laying the cards on the table, let's see what the others have got." This is why we chose this as the title for the first book in this small trilogy of Decimal Dice.

One reason for this translation is that Dice were closely associated with Gambling, yet also intimately connected with trust in the Divinities.

If the Gods did not like you, you had no chance, so in this sense the casting of the Die is a form of total release of the problem into the lap of the Gods. But have the Gods decided the outcome, or does the way we play the game determine their favour or otherwise? An eternal question.

Decimal Dice Workbook

Decimal Dice Study Course:

There are a number of book in the Decimal Dice Series that contain essential information. If you are to make the best use of **Advanced Games** you will need to go back and read "Let the Dice Fly High" as well as "Pythagorean Trines". Please Note: The prior section of this book, *Pythagorean Trines*, contains the necessary interpretations for all the aspects in this book. (Composite and Trine Interpretations)

Advanced Games itself is a compilation of the more complex Divinity Dice Games. If you can get through this section and grasp what is contained in it, you will be well equipped to cast dice for Divination in almost any situation. In fact, you could make a living from it.

However, this book is just the start of things. After you master using the 10 Sided Dice, there are whole new worlds awaiting you with Divinity Dice. This is where we use the full range of Platonic Solids as Dice. The extraordinary systems contained in the full Divinity Dice range are very specific, very powerful and very targeted.

In Rome the House of the Vestal Virgins was a gathering point for Patrician wives, who would meet and cast dice as a form of fortune telling.

Casting Dice as a form of Divination has a long history. It was seen as a way of interpreting the Will of the Gods in any given situation. Quite simply a "lucky" role of the Dice meant the Gods favoured you.

The Pythagoreans went a little further than most, and applied mathematics to research what they called "The Dice of the Gods". They gathered information about Number, and interpreted what each number combination meant.

And it still works today. Ask any question, cast the Dice, and you will get a definite and clear answer that relates directly to your situation.

In this section of Decimal Dice, **Advanced Dice Games,** we are looking at more complex ways to find interpretations. It will take time to master these, but when you do, you will be amazed at how detailed and specific the answers that come to you will be. In all, these systems are remarkably accurate when you understand and work them properly.

From the FIRST unto the SECOND where

www.numberharmonics.org

Decimal Dice Workbook

Simple Addition... (Or Pythagorean Addition)

Divinity Dice is an extraordinary development that has taken over 25 years of research and extensive unearthing of ancient documents to resolve. We have spent thousands of hours compiling and reconstructing the essential elements of the Pythagorean Schools into this modern, accessible format.

In your practice of Divinity Dice there are basic things to learn. Primarily there is the base line technique that is used in every section of the book... This is a process called: SIMPLE ADDITION..

This is the way Pythagoreans compiled Number down to their Core Elements. It is simple to do, and gives simple answers. But simple does not mean unsophisticated. The reasoning and mathematics behind this is quite complex and detailed in a study called "Vedic Math".

In a nutshell, all numbers follow specific patterns, and adding number to itself in an "Add down" fashion reveals the main pattern at work. This is all part of Vedic Math. (Which uses "Songs" or Sutras rather than multiplication or division to get answers to complex equations.)

How Simple Addition works is, as the name implies, simple. Add numbers together to form a composite number, or a first addition. EG: You may have the numbers 5, 7, 8, 3 and 9 in a series of Dice Throws. This all adds to 5+7+8+3+9 = 32. This is the COMPOSITE Number from the addition of all the numbers shown on the dice. Add this down to (3+2 = 5) and we find FIVE is the Fadic (fate) Number

Let's practice working out the numbers from three "pretend" throws of a ten sided dice: Throw the dice Six times. We get 4, 6, 7, 0, 9, 1 and the next throw is 5, 8, 2, 1, 8, 2 and the final throw is 6, 2, 9, 3, 1, 1. These add to:
- **4 + 6 + 7 + 0 + 9 + 1 = 27** (Composite) Then; **2 + 7 = 9** (Fadic)
- **5 + 8 + 2 + 1 + 8 + 2 = 26** (Composite) Then; **2 + 6 = 8** (Fadic)
- **6 + 2 + 9 + 3 + 1 + 1 = 22** (Composite) Then; **2 + 2 = 4** (Fadic)

Firstly look up your additions in the COMPOSITE Interpretations. Secondly look up in the second addition in the FATE or FADIC Interpretations. That's Simple Addition! It really IS simple. Add up the numbers then look up the interpretation for your roll of the Dice. That's it! You are, pardon the pun, ready to ROLL.

The THIRD must then Appear (Paracelsus)

www.numberharmonics.org

Decimal Dice Workbook

The MATRIX MAP

Introduction to the Pythagorean Matrix used in Decimal Dice
Techniques / Interpretations / Problem Solving Concepts

MATRIX MAP TECHNIQUE

- SERVICE / COMPASSION
- MENTAL
- EMOTIONAL
- PHYSICAL
- SUCCESS / DESIRE
- BUSINESS / CREATIVE
- AMBITION / GOALS
- ALTRUISM / IDEALS

On the following pages we will see how this simple "Matrix Map" can be used for an extraordinarily insightful understanding of our self and our environment.. The Matrix Map is a problem solving tool like no other because it helps you qualify your questions and guides you to an answer. Remember to look at the DVD to see how it all works using step by step graphics.

From the FIRST unto the SECOND where

www.numberharmonics.org

Decimal Dice Workbook

The Matrix Map Reading Game: Extended

The Matrix is a form of Divination that closely follows the principles and practices of the Pythagorean School.

We use the basic Matrix Map (shown on the previous page) and follow what we call the "Lines of Force" according to their traditional polarities. The working graph for this on the previous page you can copy and re-use without need for permission:

The ORDER in which you write down your throws of the Dice is important. Starting from the bottom left corner and running up to the top left corner, throw your TEN SIDED DICE three times. Write the number value shown in the box.

LEFT Column: Let's say you threw 5, then 7, then 9. The 5 goes into the bottom left box, the 7 goes into the middle left box and the 9 goes into the top left box. (See on following page)

MIDDLE Column: Next you throw 2, 4 and 0 ... 2 goes into the middle bottom box, 4 goes into the central box, and 0 goes into the centre top box.

Auxerre Kore

RIGHT Column: Do this for the next three throws in the right hand boxes... say it is 3, 9 and 1. 3 goes into the right bottom box. 9 goes into the right middle box and 1 goes into the right top box.

This means we now have a map that looks like what you see to the following page. Over the page we have placed the dice into their appropriate "boxes" and put in the appropriate additions. We add the various rows and write the additions into the Box allocated for this. We add all the horizontal, vertical and diagonal rows, and place them in the appropriate box

We now add the initial additions together with Simple Addition to get to a single number. Simple Addition is covered on Page Five. If you get confused, reread this page.

These rows are all added separately on the vertical, horizontal and diagonal axis, as follows: (Graphic next page)

The THIRD must then Appear (Paracelsus)

Decimal Dice Workbook

NB: Details on this technique at www.divinitydice.com

MATRIX MAP EXAMPLE:

Add each group of three numbers in the horizontal, vertical and diagonal axis to get a total addition. This addition then adds down to a single number.

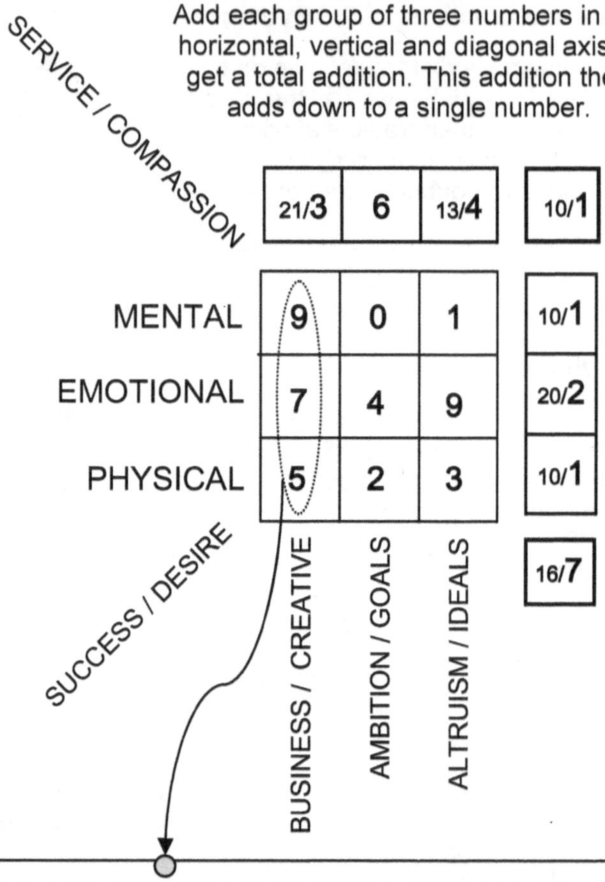

SERVICE / COMPASSION axis (diagonal ↘): 21/3, 6, 13/4, 10/1

	BUSINESS / CREATIVE	AMBITION / GOALS	ALTRUISM / IDEALS	
MENTAL	9	0	1	10/1
EMOTIONAL	7	4	9	20/2
PHYSICAL	5	2	3	10/1
				16/7

SUCCESS / DESIRE axis (diagonal ↗)

Business / Creative:	5+7+9 = 21 2+1 = **3**	Physical:	5+2+3 = 10 1+0 = **1**
Ambition / Goals:	2+4+0 = 6	Emotional:	7+4+9 = 20 2+0 = **2**
Altruism / Ideals:	3+9+1 = 13 1+3 = **4**	Mental:	9+0+1 = 10 1+0 = **1**
Success / Desire:	5+4+1 = 10 1+0 = **1**	Service / Compassion:	9+4+3 = 16 1+6 = **7**

From the FIRST unto the SECOND where

Decimal Dice Workbook

How to Interpret the Matrix Map

Remember the question you had before throwing the dice? Now look at all the aspects and shades that this question relates to. Looking at the archetypal meaning for each "line" we take the interpretation for the additions that come from the Dice throws, and see how it fits in. For Example: Let's say that you asked "How can I resolve the sense of frustration I feel?"

The Physical says "ONE". This can mean look at yourself, look at how you have your one-ness in order. Always look up the general meaning, and keep it in mind as you move onto the next line.

The Emotional says "TWO". This can indicate that your emotions are running in two or more streams of feeling. It can mean many things but essentially a Two indicates a division of some sort..

The Mental says "ONE". Are you too solitary and too single minded?

Your Business/Creative says "THREE". This indicates you perhaps need to plan things and allow your creative energy to flow more. Maybe you need to take up poetry? Three is Planning and Creativity.

The Ambition / Goals say "SIX". This is the number of Family, Business and Intuition, so perhaps it is saying look at your goals here?

The Altruism / Ideals say "FOUR". This tends to indicate a need for stability. Because of the AREA the number falls it may be that you been too generous with your time helping others and not getting a real return from this? Maybe you need to take stock of your ideals?

Your Success / Desire states "ONE". Another One! You have Three Ones, which means the ONE is the significant energy and the One is associated with Vitality and being physically active. Maybe the issue of your frustration (the question being asked) is simply that you are not being active enough. Perhaps you are not getting your physical energy moving, and you are blocking yourself because of this.

Your Service / Compassion states "SEVEN". In the area of where you connect with others, the Seven is throw. Perhaps you being too secretive? Are you being too insular? Do you need to be more social?

OVERALL: Now what we do is to add ALL the numbers throw to get an Overview or Ruling Number. 5, 7, 9, 2, 4, 0, 3, 9 and 1 all add to

Decimal Dice Workbook

40. Look up Forty in the Composite Numbers to get the overview of the reading: Which indicates ... **self containment, and possible isolation as needed, to work out the inner questions.**

From this we can deduce some difficulty on the horizon. You will need to be more physically active, to get out there and be less "internal". Maybe find a hobby or interest that takes up your energy and your attention. Get the idea? Create a story from the numbers, and it is amazing how easily it builds to a solution to the question you have.

In all, you have NINE throws of the Ten Sided Dice. Using the numbers from these throws you place them into the Matrix Map, then add up all the "lines" in this map... Eight in all. Place the simple addition of the three numbers from each line into the box provided, and look up the meaning of that number... Then INTERPRET what you see. That is both the easy and the hard part, but as you practice this simple technique you will get the idea. The answers you get will astound you with their uncanny accuracy.

ADDITIONAL STUDIES:

There are deeper aspects to the Matrix Map, regarding Trines and Double Numbers (Doublets). We cover some of these in this section.

OVERLAY MATRIX (Page 122)

You often can get a more accurate understanding of a situation using an Overlay Matrix. We give a more detailed explanation at Page 125 of this book. It is a very interesting "added" area.

We shortly will deal with the Matrix, which is, of itself, very ancient. It looks like Tic Tac Toe, but each position in it represents a Number. This adds a extra dimension to your understanding of the Dice.

DOUBLE NUMBERS: (Doublets are at Page 111)

Further, each cast of the dice places a Number over a Number. IE: in the previous example we placed a FIVE over the "One" position. This creates a 1/5 relationship. This area falls into advanced studies, and we will not be going deeply into it at this stage. Page 108 starts a brief description and interpretation for double numbers. (Doublets)

From the FIRST unto the SECOND where

Decimal Dice Workbook

Explanation of the MATRIX Pattern

This simple "Tic Tac Toe" Image has been used with variations over thousands of years. The Romans used this pattern in a game called **Terni Lapilli.** Research shows that King Solomon appears to have used a similar system when casting about for ways on how to deal with problems in his Kingdom. In fact, one of his famous rings had the "Matrix" energy pattern, which describes the basic concept for this technique.

Underneath we see a graphic that describes the "Lines of Force" that are at work within the basic shape of the King Solomon's Ring. *Below Right, this graphic is superimposed over the Matrix Graphic.*

We can go into deeper levels with this pattern. We can twist it within itself to provide Magic Square Patterns, which are the basis of Decimal Mathematics and Ratio and we can superimpose the King Solomon Ring Pattern at 45 degrees to give us the Compass Points. All sorts of Mathematical and Geometric things can be done here but for the purpose of this book we are keeping it light.

If you want to look into the Sacred Geometry more, read the book of this name by Robert Lawlor. It comes highly recommended as a starting point for those interested in Sacred Geometry.

For now we will remain with how the Pythagoreans viewed the above, which came to us in the form of what is called the MATRIX.

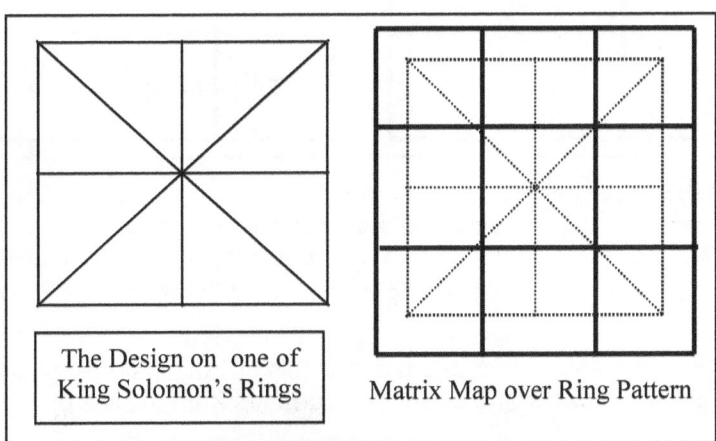

The Design on one of King Solomon's Rings

Matrix Map over Ring Pattern

The THIRD must then Appear (Paracelsus)

Decimal Dice Workbook

The Patterns you saw in the previous pages come directly from the Pythagorean Tradition, but for the present please understand that there is a lot more to it than the simple "Tic Tac Toe" pattern.

We can extend this technique in a number of directions, and gain ever deeper insight into whatever the question we may hold in our thoughts, however we are starting to get into practitioner areas where we need detailed and intimate knowledge with what the various interactions with number may mean.

Looking at the ORDER of Number in the Matrix

To give you some idea, in the basic Matrix Graph as follows there are Placements for specific numbers. It is a simple, stated order of number and the number you throw that goes OVER that number position also has an interaction. We include a small section on "Doublets" or Dual Number meanings if you care to play around with this notion.

Below is the basic "Shape" of the Matrix. To far right of this graphic are the basic Numbers positions given to each of the Nine "Squares" in the Matrix shape.

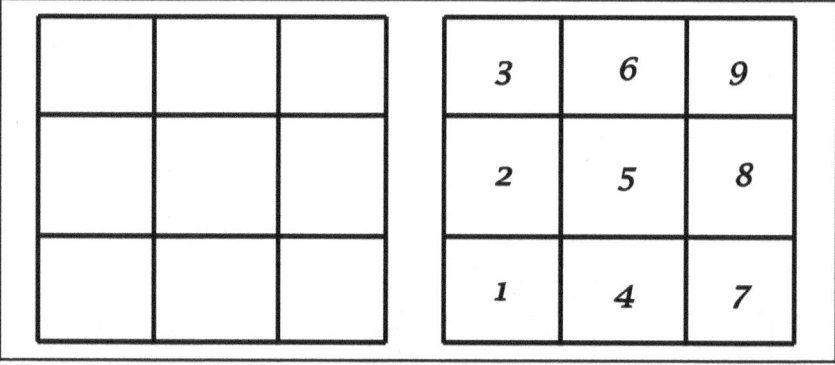

What this means if that you have a 5 thrown into the first position, the position of the ONE, then there is an interaction between the One and the Five. As I have said, when we get to this level of depth, we will need a trained practitioner to make sense of what we are throwing with the Dice.

I might add, if you cannot afford to buy this package, simply getting Nine pieces of paper and writing the numbers Zero to Nine on them,

From the FIRST unto the SECOND where

Decimal Dice Workbook

then selecting them from a hat ... this will give you the same effect as throwing the dice.

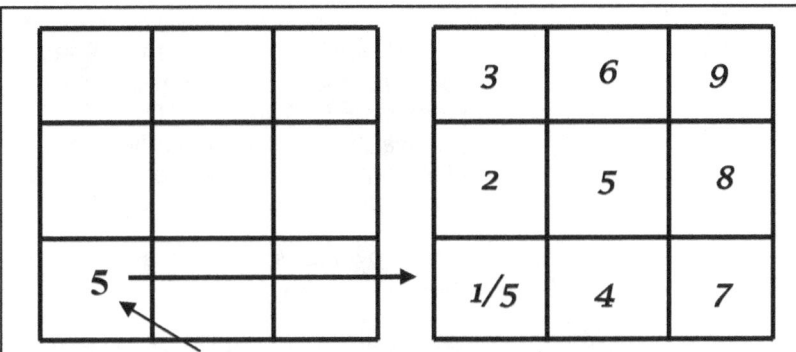

When you throw **FIVE** on the first throw you write the number 5 into the first box of your "Matrix". This gives a 1/5 interpretation for this box. Likewise, each subsequent throw goes into its own

If you want to understand the interaction between the thrown number and the number position, look up the section on Double Numbers, or Doublets, starting at Page 111 of this book. In this example, if you have thrown a FIVE at the Number One position, it indicates that there is a One/Five relationship in this area. This simply means an issue with Ego needs to be resolved before you can move forward.

The study of Number never stops, and gets more and more detailed the more you get into it. Did you know that can even convert the numbers thrown by the die to Harmonic Patterns and then play the "Music" of the Divinity Dice? Did you know that Mozart used to compose this way?

More information can be found at laddertothemoon.com.au (where you can order the numerology course, the Book of Number) and an enormous background of information at www.numberharmonics.org (Which has Pythagorean Information) if you wish to follow up more on an actual study of Number.

For the present, what you need to do is simply get used to the ideas we present here. Play with the Matrix Map, and get familiar with it. The process can be used at any time for any reason, to help answer any questions you or your friends may have.

Decimal Dice Workbook

Finding the TRINE in the MATRIX:

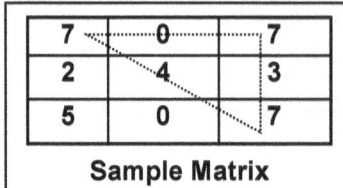

Sample Matrix

*O*ccasionally you will construct a Matrix Map where the same number will repeat three times in the Nine throws of the Ten Sided Dice. This is HIGHLY significant and indicates that the reading is under the energy of the particular Trine that is highlighted.

I will give a simple example. You throw the Matrix Map as follows: 5, 2, 7, 0, 4, 0, 7, 3, 7 (Matrix to right)

Now, in the area where the Matrix Outline from the previous page shows that where the 3, 7 and 9 positions are, the Number SEVEN has been repeated 3 times. This means that you have a relationship or TRINE based on the same number occurring three times. This Trine is interpreted as a 3-7-9 Trine because the repeating number appears over those "Boxes" that represent these numbers.

You have a 3-7-9 Trine active in this Matrix Map, and this becomes essential in understanding the deeper aspects of the question you are asking. I note further that while the Zero's in the Matrix Map don't count for anything in the additions of each line, if you throw 3 Zeros, it DOES matter as it then becomes an important TRINE.

Get the idea here? You always have the additions of the various numbers, and the meanings that come from these, but occasionally you ALSO have a Trine that emerges from the number patterns. There are other variations to understanding the Matrix Map, but it gets too complicated to convey the ideas with words, and besides this a person needs a good deal of experience before they can move onto the higher levels of subtlety within this area of Divinity Dice.

We can go over this again, let's say your throw brought up the numbers below, simply a ZERO where the FIVE was. This creates a different TRINE. In this particular case, the 3 Sevens form the 3-7-9 Trine, and now we have 3 Zeros that form a 1-4-6 Trine. We give the example of this variation in the graphic to your right..

7	0	7
2	4	3
0	0	7

Sample Matrix Map "B"

From the FIRST unto the SECOND where

www.numberharmonics.org

Decimal Dice Workbook

PRACTISE EXERCISE:

As an exercise, go through a practice interpretation, and look up the numbers in the box below. First find the Composite in the Composite Number Interpretations (at Page 36) then look up the Two Trines noted in *Pythagorean Trines*. (1-4-6 & 3-7-9)

Please try asking different "pretend" questions to see how the answer appears to change in relation to each question asked.

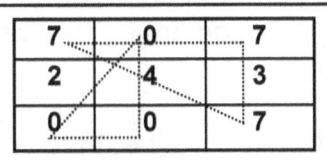

Sample Matrix Map "B"

Here we will see the Number Additions for the Sample Matrix Map "B". This example to the right is a more condensed layout than what we use on previous pages, yet as you go through it, you will find it is really the same thing.

Business / Creative:	9	Emotional:	9
Ambition / Goals:	4	Mental:	14 / 5
Altruism / ideals:	17 / 8	Success / Desire:	11
Physical:	7	Service / Compassion:	18 / 9
TRINE: (Seven's)	3-7-9	TRINE: (Zero's)	1-4-6

An Ancient Game

Two girls in Ancient Rome are playing the dice game of Tali.

This is one of the earlier dice games, and is where the game of knucklebones comes from.

The Dice were knucklebones called "Astragali". This can be seen in the image and is thrown in the same way the Game of Knucklebones is used today; from the hand, to the back of the hand, and seeing what falls to the floor.

The THIRD must then Appear (Paracelsus)

It is now time to take a rest, and look at revising what you have learned with the Matrix.

So much of what you will learn with the Dice is related to the Matrix and the various concepts that comes from it. You need to really get a grip on this ancient pattern of Nine Squares before you move ahead.

The Section of Doublets which starts on the next page is fairly straightforward, but when you get to the Advanced Study of the Matrix, you need to be well grounded in all that has come before. Otherwise, it will be water over the rim of the glass.

Decimal Dice Workbook

Double Numbers (Doublets)

In many areas of the Dice readings you will find TWO numbers seem to stand out. This is not as powerful an aspect as a Trine, or as clear an aspect as a Composite Number, but it can have significance and is included here as an add on to the basic principles of Divinity Dice. The chart of all possible combinations between One and Nine is below.

1/1	1/2	1/3	1/4	1/5	1/6	1/7	1/8	1/9
2/1	2/2	2/3	2/4	2/5	2/6	2/7	2/8	2/9
3/1	3/2	3/3	3/4	3/5	3/6	3/7	3/8	3/9
4/1	4/2	4/3	4/4	4/5	4/6	4/7	4/8	4/9
5/1	5/2	5/3	5/4	5/5	5/6	5/7	5/8	5/9
6/1	6/2	6/3	6/4	6/5	6/6	6/7	6/8	6/9
7/1	7/2	7/3	7/4	7/5	7/6	7/7	7/8	7/9
8/1	8/2	8/3	8/4	8/5	8/6	8/7	8/8	8/9
9/1	9/2	9/3	9/4	9/5	9/6	9/7	9/8	9/9

When you are playing with the Pythagorean Matrix, the numbers you throw with the dice will fall over pre-existing Number positions. This is the main use of the Pythagorean Doubles.

This is a very old game, and while the interpretations we give here are very brief, if you care to purchase at some point the Full Book of Interpretations through Divinity Dice (divinitydice.com.au) you will discover how far you can go with this simple idea. All in all, it is fun, quick and simple. A great party game.

We give here a SUMMARY of the basic interpretations for all the Double Numbers. As you go through these, please keep in mind this in not a complete summary, but an "on the fly" insight designed purely for entertainment and amusement.

Even so, the answers you will get will surprise! Treat it lightly, and just practice with the idea of getting used to the MATRIX pattern that looks like "Noughts and Crosses" or "Tic Tac Toe" as some call it.

The THIRD must then Appear (Paracelsus)

www.numberharmonics.org

Decimal Dice Workbook

Finding Doublets in the Matrix:

3	6	9
2	5	8
1	4	7

On the Left we see the traditional Number Positions in the Pythagorean Matrix. Each throw of the Dice places a number "over" the top of the pre-existing position. Below we compare the Basic Numbers against an invented throw of the dice.

Traditional Positions

3	6	9
2	5	8
1	4	7

+

The Numbers Thrown

9	2	1
7	1	1
3	0	6

=

This means we have a combination of Double Numbers as follows:

    3/9 6/2 9/1
    2/7 5/1 8/1
    1/3 4/0 7/6

NOTE: 4/0 does not count

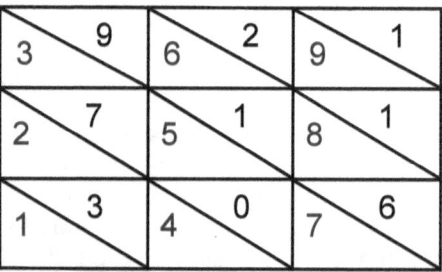

We now have a PATTERN OF NUMBER to work with. Always, when we are working with the Dice, we are looking for a pattern that relates to one or more of the interpretations.

The Next stage is to simple look up the meanings of these, and see how the picture forms. These numbers naturally form from lowest to highest for both order and convenience.

On the following page we give a brief insight on how this works.

From the FIRST unto the SECOND where
www.numberharmonics.org

Decimal Dice Workbook

Double Number Casting Interpretation:

1/3 **Big plans, but are you insecure? Just go for it.**
2/7 **Balance the Masculine and Feminine within**
3/9 **Take care with appearing pretentious**
4/0 (Just the general meaning for the Four)
5/1 Ego whispers the most cunning truth. Double check the facts.
6/2 **Can you see yourself in the mirror?**
7/6 **Get over the hump and the new day awaits**
8/1 **Throw caution to the wind,** but carefully
9/1 **Knowing what to say is half the battle**

Can you see how clearly a message is formed as these Doubles Interlink with the Matrix?

Note also that with the combination of three ONE's in the position of the 5, 8 and 9 this forms a TRINE on the 5-8-9 which we can look up and see the meaning and how it fits the above:

3/9	6/2	(9/1)
2/7	(5/1)	(8/1)
1/3	4/0	7/6

Trine Forms on the One's

5-8-9 Trine: If Wishes were Horses, Beggars would Ride. There is little Joy in an Ivory Tower.

The picture is clear, and from a random throw of the Dice we are being told to get over our pretensions and get past whatever is blocking us at this point.

Try it... Ask a question, throw the dice, and see what comes of it. First, and always, ASK YOUR QUESTION. Preferably, take a sheet of paper, and write it down on top of your matrix calculation.

Work out your Matrix Map, throw the 10 sided dice Nine Times and write down the numbers in order of their appearance in the boxes as we have discussed.

Working out the pattern of number we then go to the Interpretations for Doublets, or Double Numbers, and see what picture emerges. No matter how many times you do this, you will always find a curious new way to look at the question you have asked.

Just this process on its own is enough to solve many concerns. It's quick, easy and simple and good fun.

The THIRD must then Appear (Paracelsus)

Decimal Dice Workbook

1/1 Dominant and forthright? Choose to be You
1/2 Creative, often indecisive you ask what to do
1/3 Big plans, but are you insecure? Just go for it.
1/4 Practical and adventurous. Seize the day!
1/5 Be careful. Your Ego may want to bite you.
1/6 Trust your Intuition, but keep the wits sharp.
1/7 Embrace your Love of Life
1/8 Count the Pennies and the pounds count themselves
1/9 Possibility of great potential

2/1 Clever and cunning. Be careful of false friends.
2/2 Time to Decide. What's it to be?
2/3 Look to form new friendships
2/4 Balance the books. Someone is watching
2/5 A Secret Admirer is watching you
2/6 Beauty, appreciation and foresight can be yours
2/7 Balance the Masculine and Feminine within
2/8 Look at the new horizon before you
2/9 Rule the heart with Silence or rue the day.

3/1 Embrace the freedom, Give Joy to the World
3/2 Look at where you have been going
3/3 Plan your Day and remember the roses
3/4 Creative Tension leads to progress
3/5 Education and Instruction take you far
3/6 Mind your Mind, Care for the Heart
3/7 Freedom and Awareness come to the brave
3/8 Angular Perception of a problem often solves it
3/9 Take care with appearing pretentious

4/1 Pick up the burden and start walking
4/2 Accent the positives, reduce the negatives
4/3 What do you need to find freedom?
4/4 Don't get bogged down in detail
4/5 Step above the crowd. Be Real.
4/6 Goal setting is called for. Take stock.
4/7 Adventure and new horizons await You.
4/8 Power misused is a curse, properly applied, a blessing.
4/9 Any tick of the clock. Something is in the air.

5/1 Ego whispers the most cunning truth. Double check the facts.
5/2 Don't put your faith in beauty or politics
5/3 Feel the feeling of your own truth
5/4 Speak to trusted ones before making a decision

From the FIRST unto the SECOND where

Decimal Dice Workbook

5/5 What does your heart say? Does it speak true?
5/6 Your Path is clear. Decide right now.
5/7 Throw the habit away. Get a life worth living.
5/8 Track down the opposition. Research the facts.
5/9 Spin the weave, cast the net and catch the fish.

6/1 Pendulums find their own balance
6/2 Can you see yourself in the mirror?
6/3 Thinking is good when it serves a purpose, but how do you FEEL?
6/4 Look about, new opportunity awaits you.
6/5 Pick a safe place to roost. A storm is brewing.
6/6 Business is looking good. Write that check.
6/7 You'll have to juggle the finances until the cycle is done
6/8 Watch for hidden enemies and false friends
6/9 Tumbling down the hill can be a fun way to travel

7/1 Know that the pattern is unfolding as it should
7/2 Be in charge, but be sure to cherish your loved ones
7/3 Find your heart and you find your freedom
7/4 Movement is to be expected. Is your passport up to date?
7/5 Trust no one except yourself
7/6 Get over the hump and the new day awaits
7/7 Risk is called for. Look to Act, Dark Secrets will be Revealed.
7/8 Take no prisoners. Set your sails and GO
7/9 Embrace this moment. Breath deep

8/1 Throw caution to the wind, but carefully
8/2 Take a moment to work out the best path
8/3 Stop planning things, get on with it
8/4 Power must be matched with compassion
8/5 Emotions may run hot. Keep a cool head.
8/6 Be careful of the Boomerang effect
8/7 Trust that the process is unfolding as it should
8/8 Stop and wait. Harvest your crop and plant some seeds.
8/9 Take Charge, Move Forward. Now is the time.

9/1 Knowing what to say is half the battle
9/2 Muttering won't solve things
9/3 Speak your Truth Carefully
9/4 Anchor the Dreams Slowly
9/5 Communicate your desires clearly
9/6 Careful consideration is called for
9/7 Take this job and shove it
9/8 Embrace the new day
9/9 Silence is Golden and Loving Silence is Divine.

The THIRD must then Appear (Paracelsus)

Decimal Dice Workbook

Connecting the Dice with your Birthdate Matrix

There is a further development we can undertake with the Pythagorean Matrix, which is associating the Matrix pattern we have resolved so far with the Dice, and connecting this to your birth date.

We will look at case studies to make this clear, as it is a difficult to grasp concept. However, when you DO get the idea, it will seem blindingly obvious (like all things Pythagorean).

Roman Dice found at Pompeii

One example I would like to use it that of a very wealthy man, who walks in "High Circles" of society. He came to us one evening, and as a fellow student of Pythagorean Studies I asked if he would like an example of the latest project (What you currently hold in your hands).

He liked the idea, and so he threw the Dice for the Matrix Pattern, asking about a court matter that he was involved in. During this exercise I decided to do some "technical" Number Analysis using his birth date and I combined this with the Dice to give a more complete picture.

The result was remarkable and absolutely definitive in the answers it gave, with such overt and clear aspects evolving from the process that the odds against it being "chance" were millions to one against. What is more, what evolved was EXACTLY what the Dice had predicted

Please understand that this is a brief inspection of Number Analysis. If you want more a course on Pythagorean Numerology is available at **laddertothemoon.com.au** If you want to really be able to "Dice with the Gods", this study is highly recommended. The website has an online practitioners course (run in hard copy for the last 14 years by the Pythagorean Guild) that is considered the best of its kind in the world.

Back to the present: Following on from the concept of DOUBLETS or Double Numbers in the Matrix we are now going to show you some ideas in regards aligning your throw of the dice to the Numbers in your Date of Birth and other important DATES in your life. A DATE is really a cycle of Cycles, and it is remarkable how it all works with the Dice.

Decimal Dice Workbook

Example of Malcolm Jones

(Obviously, we do not use a person's real name) Malcolm is a man who has done very well for himself, but he has had some serious legal problems of late. He has won a major court battle which threatened his livelihood, but now he is up against tight financial stresses.

He is fighting the good fight, but it is all uphill. He is fighting regardless, and he wants to know how it will turn out. I note Malcolm is NOT asking if he will win, he is asking about OUTCOMES. This is a good start. Why? One, he is letting things go. Two, the question is open enough to reveal more than just "Will I Win or Lose".

Using the 10 Sided Dice, Malcolm throws the following Numbers: **2, 8, 9, 5, 8, 5, 5, 5, 5** This gives us the Chart to the Right

9	5	5
8	8	5
2	5	5

The first thing we note is the remarkable odds against throwing FIVE 5's in Nine throws. These are odds worthy of winning the lottery. Besides buying a ticket, Malcolm wants to know what it means.

First and foremost, when we find SUCH a weight of a single number it makes this Number DOMINANT. What is the major characteristic of the Five? Communication. It is a time to COMMUNICATE.

Let's look at the Matrix Pattern and firstly see what the TRINES might be that have emerged. And look how many there are! TEN Trines!

| 4-6-7 Trine | 4-6-8 Trine | 4-6-9 Trine | 4-7-9 Trine | 4-8-9 Trine |
| 4-7-8 Trine | 6-7-8 Trine | 6-7-9 Trine | 6-8-9 Trine | 7-8-9 Trine |

Can you see how we got all these Trines? These are all the combinations of the positions where the Five 5's are located in the Matrix. (See Page 12 to refresh the Matrix Number Positions)

The THIRD must then Appear (Paracelsus)

Decimal Dice Workbook

Now comes the Interpretations for all 10 Trines, which we give in brief here. (Of course, this is unusual for the average throw and often we do not even get a single Trine) See Pythagorean Trines for more

4-6-7 Trine: From Darkness to Light, from one to the many to the one ... The Cycle Turns.

4-6-8 Trine: Freedom is found in the Little Things. Keep a record of your thoughts.

4-6-9 Trine: Whom do you Serve? Are you making God in Your Image?

4-7-8 Trine: The Herald of Karma. Your fate is determined by the Quality of Your Heart.

4-7-9 Trine: Climb the Sacred Stair. A Door awaits. To Breath Love is to Touch the Atoms of Life

4-8-9 Trine: Silence before the Howling Gale. Fold the Sails and wait till it is passed.

6-7-8 Trine: Patience is Needed.

6-7-9 Trine: Are you at Odds with your Mind? Look into your Heart and find the Solution.

6-8-9 Trine: Take a Moment with the Divine. A Rest between the Hurdles.

7-8-9 Trine: Your Journey to Life begins. Give to life and life returns the gift.

As you can see, simply reading through the "primers" for each of the Trines paints the picture pretty clearly. There are many "Mini Answers" here, and many ways to interpret the "How will it turn out" question. But if we were to look at things overall, we would say that Patience, riding out the storm, contemplation and keeping accurate records are the sort of things that will turn the tide in Malcolm's favour.

These lines above are simply the "lead in" lines for each of the Trines. The basic Interpretations are in Pythagorean Trines, while the full interpretations are in the next step up the line, the Divinity Dice series.

Next, we move to the Matrix Map Technique. (next page) Here we will look at the additions of each line, and then move to the interpretations for the Double Numbers. Finally we combine it with the Date of Birth.

Decimal Dice Workbook

Matrix Map Technique
Malcolm Jones Example

	BUSINESS / CREATIVE	AMBITION / GOALS	ALTRUISM / IDEALS	
SERVICE / COMPASSION	19/1	18/9	15/6	15/6
MENTAL	9	5	5	19/1
EMOTIONAL	8	8	5	21/3
PHYSICAL	2	5	5	12/3
SUCCESS / DESIRE				22/4

Business / Creative:	2+8+9 = 19 1+9 = **10 = 1**	**Physical:**	2+5+5 = 12 1+2 = **3**
Ambition / Goals:	5+8+5 = 18 1+8 = **9**	**Emotional:**	8+8+5 = 21 2+1 = **3**
Altruism / ideals	5+5+5 = 15 1+5 = **6**	**Mental:**	9+5+5 = 19 1+9 = **10 = 1**
Success / Desire:	2+8+5 = 15 1+5 = **6**	**Service / Compassion:**	9+4+3 = 16 1+6 = **7**

The THIRD must then Appear (Paracelsus)

Decimal Dice Workbook

Are you still with us and following the general idea of how it all works? It takes time to be able to relax into things, but give it some of your focus, and a little time, and you will be in charge of this soon enough.

Let's look at a quick summary of the Numbers created by this Matrix:

Business / Creative:	**ONE** *New Beginnings are being offered.*
Ambition / Goals:	**NINE** *As one door opens, another closes*
Altruism / ideals	**SIX** *Home, Intuition and Business*
Success / Desire:	**SIX** (Ditto)
Physical:	**THREE** *Look at the Goal Achieved.*
Emotional:	**THREE** (Ditto)
Mental:	**ONE** *New Beginnings are being offered.*
Service / Compassion:	**SEVEN** *Secret dreams, mystical vision*

Placing the (brief) interpretation against the Line it derives from paints the picture more fully.

Altruism and Success both share SIX, which means there is a connection between these two aspects of your life. Six indicates Home, Intuition and Business. Maybe work from home and allow your inner voice to guide you? The Physical and Emotional areas share the THREE and so these are linked as well. Three means business and creativity

This jumps to the Line of Mind, and of business and creativity. These are ruled by the One. It could be new financial beginnings. Sharing a number indicates the two areas are linked in the next cycle.

Finally we come to the Service and Compassion Line. Seven here suggests that your Secret Dreams have a chance to come true.

But what does it all MEAN? This is the hard part, because you have to find the thread that links everything with the question you ask.

Naturally this is a VERY brief look through the process, but are you getting the idea as you walk through it? This is all layer upon layer of simplicity that adds up to a very complete picture overall.

You may wish to go through the interpretations in the Composite area, and you will find that illuminating. Every step into the details we take means more complication, of course, but in time you will see the simplicity driving it all. An Important thing to remember is that this process using the Matrix is OLD. In fact, it is archaic, yet as you tune into it, you will discover how relevant and current the interpretations are.

From the FIRST unto the SECOND where

Decimal Dice Workbook

Combining Birth Matrix and Dice Matrix

Malcolm Jones was born on August 21, 1958. We write this date with the DAY first, then Month, then Year. It looks like this: **21-08-1958**

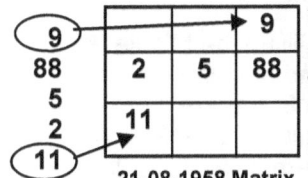

21-08-1958 Matrix

We now have the numbers **11, 2, 5, 88** and **9**. We need to "place" these in the Matrix, in order to see what the Pattern is. EG: The One goes as a 1 in the "One Box" ... There are two x 1's in the date, so we have TWO 1's in the "One Box". Similarly, there are Two 8's, so the "Eight Box" gets Two 8's in it, etc.

Obviously, according to the Graphic above, the single 2, single 5 and single 9 have one number represented. However, what is equally as important is the fact that there are VACANT boxes. In the Date of Birth of Malcolm Jones there are NO 3's, 4's, 6's or 7's present.

We find patterns according to the WEIGHT of Number in each box. We look for Numbers that all share EQUAL WEIGHT. The 2, 5 and 9 all share the same "weight. But so does the 3, 4, 6 and 7, Get the idea? They share a weight of ZERO. VACANT Numbers are ALSO important. 3 or more of the same WEIGHT form a Trine. (See Below)

		9			9			9			9			9
2	5	88	2	5	88	2	5	88	2	5	88	2	5	88
11			11			11			11			11		

2-5-9 Trine   **3-4-6 Trine**   **3-4-7 Trine**   **3-6-7 Trine**   **4-6-7 Trine**

Firstly, we have a 2-5-9 TRINE in the Date of Birth, but we also have a 3-4-6 Trine, a 3-4-7 Trine, a 3-6-7 Trine and a 4-6-7 Trine present that we derive from VACANT Numbers. Let's look at these interpretations

2-5-9 Trine: *Friends are your Greatest Resource.*
3-4-6 Trine: *Truth needs a Peg upon which to Hang.*
3-4-7 Trine: *Trim the Hedge. Over the Wall lies Yourself.*
3-6-7 Trine: *The Wolf is happiest with a Family.*
4-6-7 Trine: *From Darkness to Light ... The Cycle of Life Turns.*

Again, the story speaks for itself, but it gets more interesting when we OVERLAY the two Matrix Patterns to see what comes from a combination of the two. This requires a little rearranging of things, which we go into detail on the next page. Are you beginning to see how far you can take these simple ideas of playing with Dice?

The THIRD must then Appear (Paracelsus)

Decimal Dice Workbook

Combining the Dice with the Date of Birth

Let's re-look at the Numbers thrown by Malcolm Jones. In the same way we organized the Numbers for his Date of Birth, so too do we re-organize the Numbers from the Casting of his Dice.

		9
2	5	88
11		

Birth Matrix

		9
2	55555	88

Dice Matrix

The Five 5's Fill up the Middle "5" square, and the double 8 gets the two 8's in the "8" Square. Obviously, the single "2" and "9" go into their own square as well. To the left you can see how it all adds up.

We are dealing with the WEIGHT of Number represented. In this case only the Vacant Numbers share Equal weight, so all combination of the 1, 3, 4, 6 and 7 can be formed into Trines. There are TEN, so see if you can work them out for yourself.

		99
22	555	88
	555	88
11		

At this point we OVERLAY both of the above onto the Matrix Let's see what aspects we get when we OVERLAY the Birth Numbers with the Dice Throw. The Date of Birth over the Numbers from the cast of the dice gives us the Matrix on our left to work with. It is very simple to work out when you get used to it.

Above is the OVERLAY MATRIX. What develops is a very interesting Matrix Pattern. We have a single Trine from the BALANCED WEIGHT (of 2 numbers each) on the **One, Two** and **Nine**. This means we look up this Trine, and see what it says. Also, the VACANT NUMBERS represents a set of Trines. **3-4-6, 3-4-7, 3-6-7** and **4-6-7.**

Obviously, the VACANT TRINES repeat themselves in the Birth and Dice AND Overlay MATRIX which means that in THIS cycle, these are VERY important influences in Malcolm's life.

1-2-9 Trine: Question 101... Are you a Mouse or a Lion?
3-4-6 Trine: Truth needs a Peg upon which to Hang.
3-4-7 Trine: Trim the Hedge. Over the Wall lies Yourself.
3-6-7 Trine: The Wolf is happiest with a Family.
4-6-7 Trine: From Darkness to Light, from one to the many to the one ... The Cycle Turns until you grasp who and what you are.

Now it is simple. Can you see how the above forms a picture? It is saying "Get past your barriers" for one.. We have aimed only to give you a starting point. For more go to: www.**laddertothemoon.com.au**

Decimal Dice Workbook

RECAP: Matrix Map Method

Let's go over it all once again. When you get the hang of working with this system, and when you get familiar with what each number means, it is a remarkably quick and easy technique you can use anywhere. If you have a sheet of paper and a pen, you can be a star at the next party and really impress people.

What is more, you can really HELP people using this technique. It is SO succinct and to the point, and it gets there so quickly, that many people tend to think it is bordering on magic.

(If you get good at this basic technique, you are welcome to go to the web at **www.divinitydice.com.au** and register for a practitioner test.)

3	6	9
2	5	8
1	4	7

The Basic Pattern never really varies. You, or your client, has a question that needs an answer. The 10 Sided Dice is used. Throw the Dice NINE TIMES and the numbers thrown are put into the Matrix Square in the sequence of Number Order as shown on your Left.

If the throws are: 1, 3, 5, 7, 5, 9, 1, 8 and 2. This means the Matrix Square will look like the Square to your Right. We then ADD EACH LINE according to the Matrix Map on Page 15. This gives the additions for each line as:

5	9	2
3	5	8
1	7	1

Business / Creative:	1+3+5 = 8	**Physical:**	1+7+1 = 9
Ambition / Goals:	7+5+9 = 21 2+1 = 3	**Emotional:**	3+5+8 = 16 1+6 = 7
Altruism / Ideals:	1+8+2 = 11 1+1 = 2	**Mental:**	5+9+2 = 16 1+6 = 7
Success / Desire:	1+5+2 = 8	**Service / Compassion:**	5+5+1 = 11 1+1 = 2

Now, without knowing what the question is, we can see that certain Lines share the same addition. Both the Emotional and Mental Line add to 16. Both the Altruism and Service Lines add to 11. Both the Business and Success Lines add to 8. *This means there is a clear connection between these pairs of Lines.* Now, obviously, the type of question asked will determine exactly what this connection may be. And always remember, the right question gives you the best answer.

The THIRD must then Appear (Paracelsus)

Decimal Dice Workbook

You can look up the meaning for the Trines in the "Pythagorean Trines" section. We are not working out the Meaning or Interpretation of this throw, but simply going through the process as an exercise.

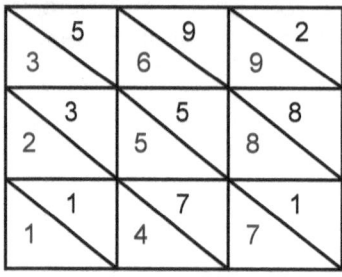

Next we move to the **Double Numbers**, which in this instance gives us the graph we see to the Left. This pattern gives us the number combinations as follows:

1/1, 2/3, 3/5, 4/7, 5/5, 6/9, 7/1, 8/8, 9/2

We look these combinations up in the Double Numbers to reveal the "Story" they are telling us.

	6	99
22	5	
1		

25-09-1962

We then take a further step of looking at the Birth Date. Work out the Matrix for this, then lay this OVER your Matrix for the Dice throw. We call it the **Overlay Matrix**. Let's say the Birth Date for the person asking the question is 25/09/1962. This gives the Matrix to your right.

The Birth Matrix gives us a series of Trines. Numbers that occur in equal proportion are always connected. The 1, 5 and 6 share what is called the same "weight" and thus form a 1-5-6 Trine. Also note that the 3, 4, 7 and 8 are VACANT, therefore these too paradoxically share EQUAL WEIGHT. This gives a series of Trines that derive from the combinations of these numbers. 3-4-7, 3-4-8, 3-7-8, 4-7-8 are all TRINES in this Date of Birth.

5	9	2
3	5	8
1	7	1

Dice Matrix

3		9
2	55	8
11		7

Dice Matrix done as Birth Matrix

Tricky? It gets worse! To the Left is the Dice we cast placed into the form of the Birth Matrix. At first this is difficult to understand, but in a nutshell we place the Numbers from our throw into a Matrix just as we have done in the above BIRTH Matrix. Then look at the Trines that evolve from working out the Matrix for the Throw of the Dice we find the pattern we show BELOW the original Matrix.

Here we find LOTS of Tines emerge. The 2, 3, 7, 8 and 9 all share EQUAL WEIGHT and so there are Trines between all of these numbers. These are: 2-3-7, 2-3-8, 2-3-9, 2-7-8, 2-7-9, 2-8-9, 3-7-8, 3-7-9, 3-8-9, 7-8-9.

*Go to **www.divinitydice.com.au** website for more information.*

Decimal Dice Workbook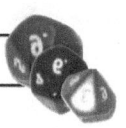

OVERLAY MATRIX EXAMPLE

Now we set p the Overlay Matrix. We combine the Birth Matrix with the Dice Matrix we have just worked out (previous page). This gives us a pattern as follows. (Here we show you the "split" version and how it goes to the Overlay Matrix)

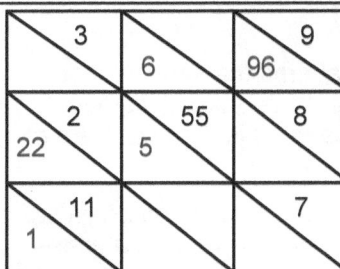

	6	99
22	5	
1		

Birth Matrix

+

3		9
2	55	8
	11	7

Dice Matrix

=

3	6	999
222	555	8
111		7

OVERLAY

This graph shows you the Birth Matrix in the lower left corner and the Dice Matrix in the Upper Right corner of each "square" of the Table.

We take the Birth and Dice Matrix and put all the numbers together to get the OVERLAY MATRIX. In this Overlay Matrix we find that the 1, 2, 5 and 9 share EQUAL WEIGHT. We also find that the 3, 6, 7 and 8 all share EQUAL WEIGHT. A Trine is formed between all numbers that share equal weight.

In the above example we can see that are many Trines are created. Within this particular Overlay Matrix we find the following Trines: (Below)
1-2-5, 1-2-9, 1-5-9, 2-5-9, 3-6-7, 3-6-8, 3-7-8 and 6-7-8

Map of Possible Trines in Overlay Matrix

To your Left we see a Graphic of all the combinations of Trines in the Overlay Matrix for the Date of Birth and the Casting of the 10 Sided Dice.

As you can easily see, a lot of information can evolve from a simple throwing of the Ten Sided Dice.

Obviously, from this point on it is simply a matter of getting familiar with the meanings of the trines and how they interact. What is now clear is that there is a LOT to understand from just this one Technique. Of course, for more info go to the website at **www.divinitydice.com.au**

The THIRD must then Appear (Paracelsus)

Decimal Dice Workbook

Summary of Matrix Map Technique

This *is a very detailed and complex section of Decimal Dice, but if you really take the time to study this and get into it the results will absolutely amaze you. Just this Technique alone will earn a person who wishes to use it professionally an income for life. Imagine being able to travel anywhere in the world with just a drawing pad, a small book, and a Ten Sided Dice and be able to make a living!*

The Matrix is an ancient tool for Divining the Patterns that will affect our future. As you get familiar, and this takes many years, you will hardly look at a book or any reference, because the patterns in the Matrix are a book unto themselves.

On this journey of discovery you will be surprised and delighted again and again, because every single person who comes to you with a question will show you another aspect of the Matrix you may not have yet considered. It is a never ending story.

We will seek to constantly update the website at *divinitydice.com.au* as more examples and information comes to hand, and you are invited to go there at any time. If you wish to practice professionally, we will set you a test. If you pass, you will be registered as a member of the Pythagorean Guild as a Divinity Dice practitioner.

Next we move onto the last of the major techniques of this workbook, which is the Past, Present, Future Technique.

Cleromancy Board with Casting pieces and Dice

Divination techniques with Dice is called Cleromancy which is used all over the world in various ways.

To the Left is a recreation of an ancient Germanic system using Dice, stones, counters and knucklebones on a leather "Matrix"

From the FIRST unto the SECOND where

www.numberharmonics.org

Decimal Dice Workbook

The PAST, PRESENT, FUTURE Game:

Everyone wants to know something about the future. What lies ahead? It is normal and natural to have a curiosity about what is to come, but really, when we understand better what has gone, and what is now, then we are far better placed to comprehend what is to come.

There are many different ways to play the Ten Sided Divinity Dice game, and this is a very simple and effective method that will give you answers to your questions quickly and easily.

Obviously, you have to have a question, and you must ask it before you roll your dice. But be careful of the type of question you ask, because it has a bearing on what will come through for you.

EG: Questions like "Is this relationship going to work?" is really very non-specific, and you will get a fairly non-specific answer as a result. Maybe this is what you want, but consider shaping the question more than the "shotgun" approach of the Yes or No type response.

Learn to Sniper with your questions. Learn to really target exactly what it is that you want to know. This is an art unto itself, and it takes some practice, but consider. You have met someone, you like them, but is there something there in the long term? More to the point, in every relationship there is something to learn, so maybe shift the focus to this consideration "What am I to learn from the connection with so and so?"

Or perhaps, "What am I to give to so and so?" Better still... "What is the Physical, Emotional and Spiritual lessons I have to learn and share with this relationship?" Can you see how this type of approach gives you far more to work with? Whatever the question, just keep it in mind as you throw the dice.

Getting the right question is often the hardest part. After that, all we do is throw the 10 Sided Dice, and write down the numbers that show up. That's it! Write down the numbers into the allocated boxes. You might like to be tricky and write them from the lowest to the highest number, and this can be useful in later developments of the game. However, for the moment just place the number thrown into the grid outlined. *(Grid shown on opposing page)*

Decimal Dice Workbook

Present, Past, Future Game Graph

1ˢᵀ Dice	2ⁿᵈ Dice	3ʳᵈ Dice	1ˢᵗ Addition	2ⁿᵈ Addition	3ʳᵈ Addition	
						PRESENT
Summary Line →						
						PAST
Summary Line →						
						FUTURE
Summary Line →						

The Past Present Future Game is essentially 3 x 3 x 3 throws of the 10 sided Die which are added in a step by step fashion to generate a "field of Number" that give a significant Interpretation to the questioner

From the FIRST unto the SECOND where

Decimal Dice Workbook

I stress that it is VERY important to follow the steps exactly as shown in the diagrams. If you do, it will be obvious and simple to understand. There are three main sections, Present, Past and Future. Each of these sections hold THREE THROWS of your three 10 Sided Dice. In all, there are NINE THROWS of the three 10 sided dice.

Let's take a closer look to show how we use the work grid on the facing page. It looks complex, but it is really quite simple.

To your Left is the Working Grid for the Past, Present, Future Game. We have a position for the number values of each casting of the dice under the 1st, 2nd, and 3rd Dice areas. We have the position for Additions to the right of these. At the far right we have the position for the Final Additions under the headings of Present, Past and Future.

Go through the following pages slowly, and it will become clear fairly readily how to work with all of this. It looks a little complicated, but it really is fairly straightforward.

The FIRST THROW of THREE

On the following page is the graphic for the first three throws, and in the graphics after this we show you the build up of the Past Present, Future Game. In all, you will have 3 x 3 x 3 throws of the Die.

Don't worry about all the boxes. It looks complex but it stays simple... The Rule is simple: Just follow the steps and you will soon get the basic idea. We will use the graphic on the opposing page for each roll of the Dice, so follow it and see what sense you make of I all. Let's pretend I have rolled the die and gotten 6, 7, and 0. What we do is to put these numbers into the first three boxes, from left to right. Then we simply add these numbers up, and put the addition of them in the "1st Addition" box. (0+6+7 = 13)

NOTE: Normally we do not put all the numbers we are adding up into the 1st Addition Box, but in this exercise I want to show you clearly where the 13 came from.

We have thrown the dice numbers of: 0, 6 and 7. Write these down (From Lowest to Highest Number) in the first set of boxes from the top Left hand side of the graphic. Add these together: 0+6+7 = 13. That's it!. 13 in the FIRST ADDITION derived from the first set of three numbers found by your first three throws of the Ten Sided Die.

Decimal Dice Workbook

Present, Past, Future Game: The First Throw

1ST Dice	2nd Dice	3rd Dice	1st Addition	2nd Addition	3rd Addition	PRESENT				PAST				FUTURE		
0	6	7	0+6+7 =13	1 + 3 = 4												

From the FIRST unto the SECOND where

www.numberharmonics.org

Decimal Dice Workbook

The next step is to use what is called "Simple Addition" and to add the 13 as One and Three. (1+3 = 4) Obviously we cannot add the Four down to anything less, so there is no 3rd addition in this case.

Let's go over it again. We write down the numbers that show on the die staring in the top left hand corner of the graph and working down in sets of three throws. We then add these up. In the first row the First Addition is 13, and we then add the 13 to the Second Addition of FOUR. We cannot reduce Four any further, and so this is the "remainder".

In all, we throw our three castings of the 10 sided dice Nine Times. This means we will have nine sets of three numbers to add up. (3x3x3)

We will be looking at this in close focus in the following pages, but as we move into this, always remember that what we are looking for are PATTERNS OF NUMBER. EG: Any Number that re-occurs 3 times or more has a significance, any 3 *different* numbers in a throw of three has a significance. It will take time to master what all this means, but as you practice it will become clear for you.

On this Page we show a reduced graphic that shows a sample Chart of the first Nine Throws. This demonstrates the FIRST STAGE of working out the Past, Present, Future Game. Here we use what we call Simple Addition. We see here how each row of numbers adds down to a Composite then to a Fadic (or Single) Number. Soon we will see how the single numbers give up a final addition to consider. Relax: It may all look complex but it really is quite simple.

Look below. Can you see how a "map" of numbers is starting to form? If we add the 4, 9 and 9 we find it adds to 22... So look up the Composite meaning for 22 to see what your Present Situation is like in regards to your question. (See *Pythagorean Trines* Workbook)

1ST Dice	2nd Dice	3rd Dice	1st Addition	2nd Add	3rd Add		
0	6	7	0+6+7 = 13	1 + 3 = 4			
6	6	6	6+6+6 = 18	1 + 8 = 9			
4	5	9	4+5+9 = 18	1 + 8 = 9			
				4+9+9 =	22	PRESENT	

The Full Graphic for the all 27 throws is on the page 133

The THIRD must then Appear (Paracelsus)

Decimal Dice Workbook

This interpretation for 22 says (In brief) that: "*New beginnings are indicated, but care should be taken to get off on the right footing.*" What was that question about a Love affair? See how it works?

Remember:: According to the QUESTION you ask, the meaning of the Interpretation will take shape accordingly.

Looking for the TRINE and the COMPOSITE:

The example on the previous page shows how we can resolve a Composite Number from a set of Three throws. NOW we start to look for Patterns and Trines in the cast of Numbers.

In this case, there is a TRINE formed in the THIRD casting because 4, 5 and 9 are all different numbers. What does this mean? Well, it 'may' mean something, but for now you just make a note of the Trine, and keep it for reference. There is NO Trine that forms from the additions of the above pattern, and it may be that no other Trine forms in all the Throws of the 10 sided die. If this were so, we count on the Composite Numbers for the interpretation.

NB: There is a "ranking" of importance with Trines. If there is a Trine in the FINAL three additions it is always important. A Trine in the Composite Additions is the next step down in importance. A Trine in the Dice Casting is of the last rank of importance.

If you get a Trine forming in the "Present" Area of the chart, it relates to where your Question is RIGHT NOW. Obviously, the Present in this addition adds to 4, 9, 9 ... Not three different numbers, therefore NOT a Trine. In the Future area, where the question may be going. In the Past area, what it comes from.

Primarily we are looking at the COMPOSITE MEANINGS that evolve into the positions of the Present, Past and Future. There is ALWAYS a Composite Number to look up... Consider the Trine as a bonus!

Please note that you will not always get a Trine (Three separate Numbers) from your additions or casting of the dice. In such cases we rely on the Composite Numbers for interpretations.

From this information we will create the "Number Map" that gives us the interpretation we are looking for. For the sake of simplicity, on Page 38 to 39 we have written down an example and placed it into a grid pattern for you: 3 x 3 x 3 throws of the 10 Sided Dice. That's it!

From the FIRST unto the SECOND where

Decimal Dice Workbook

An Ancient Pattern: Below you will see the start of the additions used in the Past, Present, Future Game. This is part of an Ancient Vedic tradition that came to the West via the Gypsy folk.

Present, Past, Future Game: 27 Throws with 1st and 2nd Additions

1st Dice	2nd Dice	3rd Dice	1st Addition	2nd Addition	3rd Addition	
0	6	7	0+6+7 = 13	1 + 3 = 4		PRESENT
6	6	6	6+6+6 = 18	1 + 8 = 9		
4	5	9	4+5+9 = 18	1 + 8 = 9		
6	7	1	6+7+1 = 14	1 + 4 = 5		PAST
4	6	6	4+6+6 = 16	1 + 6 = 7		
7	7	9	7+7+9 = 23	2 + 3 = 5		
3	1	9	3+1+9 = 13	1 + 3 = 4		FUTURE
1	8	2	1+8+2 = 11	1 + 1 = 2		
4	7	5	4+7+5 = 16	1 + 6 = 7		

All the Trines in the example are circled for ease of understanding

The THIRD must then Appear (Paracelsus)

Decimal Dice Workbook

Now we add the simple addition of these numbers. Add DOWN the additions of the 1st Addition, add DOWN the additions of the 2nd Addition. We are looking to form a COMPOSITE Number and a TRINE of Number (which is any group of three different numbers) This forms the first level of Divination. Again, remember that we do not always find three separate numbers that constitute a Trine. (Below)

Present, Past, Future Game: The First Summary

1ST Dice	2nd Dice	3rd Dice	1st Addition	2nd Addition	1st Summary	
0	6	7	0+6+7 = 13	1 + 3 = 4		PRESENT
6	6	6	6+6+6 = 18	1 + 8 = 9		
4	5	9	4+5+9 = 18	1 + 8 = 9		
			13+18+18 = 49	4+9+9 = 22	22	
					22—2=2 = 4	FOUR
6	7	1	6+7+1 = 14	1 + 4 = 5		PAST
4	6	6	4+6+6 = 16	1 + 6 = 7		
7	7	9	7+7+9 = 23	2 + 3 = 5		
			14+16+23 = 53	5+7+5 = 17	17	
					17—1=7 = 8	EIGHT
9	1	3	9+1+3 = 13	1 + 3 = 4		FUTURE
2	8	1	2+8+1 = 11	1 + 1 = 2		
4	7	6	4+7+6 = 17	1 + 7 = 8		
			13+11+17 = 41	4+2+8 = 14	14	

From the FIRST unto the SECOND where

Decimal Dice Workbook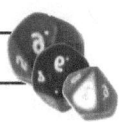

We need to understand how to make sense out of all this large "Field of Numbers". To do this we need to approach it one step at a time, and follow a simple method.

1. FIRST Step: Throw the 10 Sided Die
2. SECOND Step: Add up each set of three throws
3. THIRD Step: Add these down to their Composite Numbers
4. FORTH Step: Look up the Interpretations

EG: In the Present the Composite Number is 22, which we have already looked at. In the Past the Composite is 17 and in the Future the Composite is 14. (We can look at the first additions of 49, 53 and 41 as well, but due to space restrictions we leave this up to you)

PRESENT:
22: Behind the clown mask there is often a calculating and satirical nature.
49: *An odd, quirky period is coming up for you. You will attract odd, quirky personalities.*

PAST:
17: *This indicates that Soul will rise like the phoenix from all adversity, stronger and better for the trial.*
53: *An Important Cycle. This is a time of Harvest and Manifestation, but if you break the Laws of Silence things will reverse.*

FUTURE:
14: *A number of movement, travel and new associations.*
41: *If you are practical and reliable, this period is often found to be extremely lucky.*

As you can see, it is very easy to spot a "line of thought" from looking at the different Composite meanings for the numbers represented in the Past, Future and Present Boxes. Let's pretend the question is about WORK. We are thinking of changing our job and want to know if the new position being offered is the right way to go.

It does not take a lot of imagination to draw for yourself a story that fits the interpretations for the various numbers represented. Already we are starting to get a picture forming, based on the question that has been asked. *The Dice are saying that your new Job offers new horizons. Look for a clown, get on with them, and expect a few internal difficulties as you adjust to the new circumstance.*

The THIRD must then Appear (Paracelsus)

Decimal Dice Workbook

FINDING THE TRINE:

NOW: We look and see if we can find a Trine (A Trine constitutes Three different numbers between One and Nine). Simply add down the final numbers of 22, 17 and 14 to their FADIC (single) Numbers.

Can it be simpler? *We add down the 22 to get 4, the 17 to get 8, and the 14 to get 5.* Rearrange these numbers from Lowest to Highest (For ease of looking it up) and this gives us a **4-5-8 Trine**. On the following page we give the interpretation for the 4-5-8 Trine. We give the FULL interpretation from the Divinity Dice Book of Interpretations on the following page, but the simple interpretations from *Pythagorean Trines* are sufficient for most purposes.

Once you get an answer, reflect on what is written, always keeping in mind the question you have asked. Obviously, the nature of the question must be placed against the interpretation if we are to understand things fully

It is important to note that we do not always find a Trine of Numbers, and you may choose to recast your dice OR carry on with just the Composite Interpretations. Alternatively, look for "lesser" Trines. These "Lesser" Trines are those that occur elsewhere in your casting of the Die. EG: the 2nd Addition of the Future Zone forms a 2-4-8 Trine. Look this up, and see how it fits.

We also can look at the throws of the dice themselves, and see what Trines form. We find: 4-5-9 / 1-6-7 / 1-3-9 / 1-2-8 / 4-6-7 as we go from Top to Bottom of the graph opposite. These are circled on Page 31. Will ALL of these be significant? Well, maybe, but probably not.

ASKING THE QUESTION:

All of the above, and every aspect of this book only comes to life and has MEANING only when you Ask the Question before throwing. Questions are loosely in the categories of Love, Family, Career, Money, Relationships, Spirituality, Children and Destiny.

Our question is of Career. We have thrown the dice, and the chart to the right hand side has come up. What is the message? We have the Composite Interpretation on the previous page, so let's look at what the Dice are saying to us with the Trines! (*Remember, always refer to Pythagorean Trines for a summary of Trine Interpretations*)

From the FIRST unto the SECOND where

Decimal Dice Workbook

Finding a Trine in the Additions

1ˢᵀ Dice	2ⁿᵈ Dice	3ʳᵈ Dice	1ˢᵗ Add	2ⁿᵈ Add	Summary	
0	6	7	0+6+7 = 13	1 + 3 = 4		PRESENT
6	6	6	6+6+6 = 18	1 + 8 = 9		
4	5	9	4+5+9 = 18	1 + 8 = 9		
			13+18+18 = 49	4+9+9 = 22	2+2 = 4	FOUR
6	7	1	6+7+1 = 14	1 + 4 = 5		PAST
4	6	6	4+6+6 = 16	1 + 6 = 7		
7	7	9	7+7+9 = 23	2 + 3 = 5		
			14+16+23 = 53	5+7+5 = 17	1+7 = 8	EIGHT
9	1	3	9+1+3 = 13	1 + 3 = 4		FUTURE
2	8	1	2+8+1 = 11	1 + 1 = 2		
4	7	6	4+7+6 = 17	1 + 7 = 8		
			13+11+17 = 41	4+2+8 = 14	1+4 = 5	FIVE

We have just cast the Dice for the Past / Present / Future Game. One of the aspects we have found is a TRINE. The Interpretation for this Trine is below. (This is from the complete version available in the Divinity Dice Book of Interpretations)

4-5-8 Trine: Are You Soul with a Body, or a Body with a Soul?

If you are of a higher mind and not needing so much in the way of material goods, this aspect is positive and fortunate. It is like buying a ticket to the Higher Self. However, if you are materially minded with goals and aspirations focussed on the mundane you are being advised to watch out. Cover your back, as bad luck may well seem to dog your every move. The real answer is that you are being drawn towards your Spiritual Purpose. This must be found if peace is to settle in your heart.

Continued Over Page

The THIRD must then Appear (Paracelsus)

Decimal Dice Workbook

You may have spent your youth reading Siddhartha and the principles of the Buddha, but perhaps at some point that call of the wild animal in you caught your attention? Maybe you always wanted to experience the world and all it offered? This is good, because the Buddha, bless his cotton socks, got it wrong. Desire does not equal pain, Pain equals Desire. Salve what pains you, seek out the aches and rub them with whatever balm works for you. Find the itches you need to scratch, and scratch them. Sort it all out because in the end all that will be left is your true desire.

What is your true desire? After the apparent random walk on our own, we finally realise the flagstones are well worn, and the path is well trodden. You only thought it was the road less travelled.

Why did it seem so lonely? Mostly we get so locked into ourselves that we don't see the people at the train station. You have been working on the solution to your questions. But now finally you are waking up to the realities about you, and it is time to make a choice. Are you Soul with a body, or a body with a Soul. The answer will determine the remainder of your journey.

We all have a desire for emotional balance and material well being, but this is often frustrated by apparently endless problems. Yet if you look deeply into yourself you will find that this is because at heart you have little interest in worldly matters. It is just a matter of survival.

When you fully accept that what we do here on Earth is for survival, and thus take the stress out of being better than the next person, etc. then things will work out better in an emotional and financial sense.

This is an excellent energy if you want to be of service in the spiritual orders. You have a faithfulness and persistence that are needed for these vocations. Naturally, the reverse can be true and you can be afflicted with such traits as pessimism and selfishness. Life is a mirror. What you project is what it returns.

AN attitude of materialism comes often because the child's altruistic nature suffered embarrassment or confusion. Money and security is seen as the better option. In time you will understand that an attitude of Service to Life pats better than service to self, and needs greater inner strength. You will learn the journey can pay you a greater dividend than mere money, it can pay you with friends and happy times.

From the FIRST unto the SECOND where

Decimal Dice Workbook

When this Trine presents itself you have the opportunity to break through into the secret place inside yourself. This "Secret Place" is simply the inner self in its pure form. The eternal discovery of self (Soul) allows you to express yourself more clearly in this outer world. The beginning, the middle and the end are all part of the song we sing to ourselves. Look at the song you sing, which is really the inner attitudes we hold. The Pythagoreans said, "To become what we sing, this is the price the Gods exact for song."

Your Motto is: *The price of freedom is eternal vigilance.*

===========

So, is that it for the basic reading in this section of the Present, Past and Future? Nope, there's more!

We can easily see how, in the final additions, that a pattern of three numbers, 4, 5 and 8 have been found. We have also looked at the Composites, and found a Trine in the FUTURE area.

1 + 3 = 4	In this case the numbers 13, 11 and 17 added down to form a **2-4-8 Trine**, but we can go a little further, and add up the numbers of this Trine to see what the Composite says. As you can see by the additions to the left, the Composite Number is 14: **Snakes and Ladders: A number of movement, travel and new associations**.
1 + 1 = 2	
1 + 7 = 8	
4+2+8 = 14	

This becomes a sort of priority number for the reading. A Trine has *Emphasized* this number as being significant, and it does fit well into the notion of a new job. Going up or down? Snakes and Ladders... the fall of the Die will determine it. Movement, travel and new associations all easily to fit into a New Job question.

This is an ancient system based on what is known as the Law of Three. It is also Trigonometry. To locate anything exactly in surveying you need three reference points. This allows us to calculate the exact position of a thing in relationship to the set, fixed points.

What we are doing is, literally, creating a SURVEY of our situation. To do this accurately, we need three reference points. IE: Past, Present and Future; 27 Throws of the Die = 3 x 3 x 3 throws; Trines, etc. It is NOT a given that we will find a Trine every time we do this exercise, but we will ALWAYS find three Composites to work with.

The THIRD must then Appear (Paracelsus)

Decimal Dice Workbook

Even so, we always look to see what Trines may occur in all the Present, Past and Future additions. In the specific example of the previous pages we see a 2-4-8 Trine is formed in the FUTURE Area. Look this up and we find it says: (In brief)

2-4-8 Trine: The Seed must break through its Prison of Earth to Grow. *The Power of Growth is highlighted with this Aspect coming up. Yet a seed must break first through its own shell before it can sprout, and then it must break through the barrier of earth to reach the light.*

Now as this Trine is in the Future area, the reading appears to say that the Future is looking rosy but there is a lot of work to do to get through the early stages. That seems pretty much in accord with a new Job that is going to be significant to you. Indeed, if it were a new relationship, you may well say the same thing!

No matter the question, the Interpretations will adjust and adapt to fit into the framework being offered. Go with the flow, and it will all work out OK... Get the idea?

Please note, when doing the Trines I always re-arrange numbers so that they run from lowest to highest. This makes it easy to look up in a database, and it gives a constant format that everyone can easily agree on.

There is a simple principle behind all of Number and all studies of Number we will ever do remain true to this principle: One and One equals Two ... That's the Order of Number, and if you can believe what the Tibetans say, this is the Secret of Life itself.

From the FIRST unto the SECOND where

www.numberharmonics.org

Decimal Dice Workbook

Closing Comments

This brings us to an end of your primary Divinity Dice study: Decimal Dice: working with the 10 Sided Die.

The next level of Study is the Divinity Dice Workbook, which works hand in hand with its Sister Publication, The Book of Interpretations. These books are based on the use of the five Platonic Solids as Dice. Finally there is the follow up publication, Pythagorean Patterns.

Did you miss the primer book in the series? It is called "*Dicing Up Your Destiny*" and it is a general book that gives over 820 interpretations for every possible combination of 3 x 10 sided Dice. It's light reading and great fun at parties.

If you wish to take your studies further, Michael Wallace has also authored a course on the Study of Number. This is available through Amazon as the Book of Number Series. (laddertothemoon.com.au)

Important work that relates to the Pythagorean techniques with Sound and Music healing has been done at Number Harmonics. If you are interested in this area, go to www.numberharmonics.org

Another exciting development has been working with Gerry Bull and his extraordinary technique of teaching kids to play music. He has followed the Pythagorean Model and gets simply extraordinary results. Write to the author for more information if interested..

FURTHER STUDY and INTERESTS:

Has some of the subject matter gotten you looking for more? You can take further courses in Pythagorean Numerology and other related subjects on line. Go to **www.laddertothemoon.com.au**

You want more DICE stuff? Well, more Dice you get. Your study of the entire Pythagorean system of Dice Divination can be greatly enhanced by looking at the materials available at **divinitydice.com.au** Here you will find a whole new world of Dice Games using the Platonic Solids as well as extraordinary historical information regarding Dice.

At that site you can order the Divinity Dice Workbook, including the Book of Interpretations for all aspects found using any type of Dice.

The THIRD must then Appear (Paracelsus)

Decimal Dice Workbook

Credits:

No Man is an Island, and in producing the Divinity Dice works I have had the enormous resource (under) of the Pythagorean books from numerous authors. Let us not forget the hard advice from Dicing Savant, Luke Rhinehart. (the Diceman) (AKA George Cockcroft)

We trust you will enjoy the Dice Games and Concepts we bring you in this series and the Book of Number series.

Bust of Pythagoras

REFERENCES:

"The Pythagorean Sourcebook" by Guthrie (Thanes Press)
"Fair Dice" by Persi Diaconis and Joseph B. Keller.
 Encyclopedia Britannica
"The Egyptian Book of the Dead" by E A Wallis Budge
"The Secret Doctrine" by H P Blavatsky
"The Ten Books on Architecture" by Vitruvius
"Egypt: Myths and Legends" by Lewis Spence
"The Glory that was Greece" by J C Stobart
"Constantinople" (1906 version) Alexander Van Millingen
"The Message of the Sphinx" by Hancock and Bauval
"Metamagical Themas" Douglas Hofstadter
"The Life you were meant to Live" by Dan Millman
"Hebrew Myth" (Series): Raphael Patia and Robert Graves
"I Claudius" Robert Graves
 The Colleen McCulloch novels on Troy and Ancient Rome
"The Diceman" and "Book of the Die" Luke Rhinehart

A rare example of Roman Dice that use Roman Numerals. Normally, Roman Dice were recognized by their unique "Dot in Circle" pattern.

"If you are into Divining with Dice, you owe it to yourself to take a good look at the Divinity Dice books. A great way to exercise the mind, but beware... Excessive thinking can bring on brain strain."
 Luke Rhinehart, "The Diceman" (AKA Prof George Cockroft)

From the FIRST unto the SECOND where

Decimal Dice Workbook

More Books by the Author

If you liked the Decimal Dice Workshop, there is a whole lot more in store. Following on we have Divinity Dice (Full Five Dice Polyhedral Divination) and the Book of Interpretations.

For Pythagorean Number Analysis, there is the Book of Number Series. (pictured right) This is a complete "How to" course in Numerology and are considered by many as the best books on the subject.

 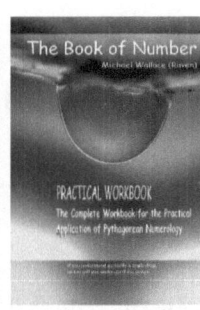

 Hello Planet Earth is a delightful Modern Myth, originally written when the author was on death's door in 1984, and only recently found in a manuscript box and published. It is an utterly delightful story, suitable to children through the grandparents. You will never see life the same way after you read this book.

Ratology is an extraordinary anthem that plays out the internal themes of the mind and emotions, putting in sharp perspective the nature of the human condition. This book has a staggering clarity in regards the bedrock of thinking and feeling most of us base out beliefs and cherished notions upon. Ratology will shatter any illusions you may hold, and reawaken you to

The THIRD must then Appear (Paracelsus)

www.numberharmonics.org

Further Information

For more information on Divinity Dice and associated products and services, please go to

www.divinitydice.com.au

This book is published under the Berne Convention. All rights are reserved. Apart from any fair dealing for the purpose of private study, research, criticism or review, as permitted under the Copyright Act, 1966, no part of this publication may be reproduced, stored in a retrieval system, or transmitted, in any form or by any means, electronic, electrical, chemical, mechanical, optical, photocopying, recording or otherwise, without the prior permission of the copyright holder. Enquiries should be send to the publishers at the under mentioned address.

ISBN: **978-0-9756994-3-0**

Copyright 2006-2015 Michael Wallace

Publisher: Ladder to the Moon (QRC Australia)
PO Box 1355 Kingscliff NSW Australia 2487

The Author of this Book is Michael Wallace. He is the founder of the Pythagorean Guild and has been writing on the subject of Numbers, Harmonics, Dice and all aspects of the Pythagorean teachings for the last 30 years.

He is a Master Musician, Bodyworker, Writer, Dice Master and author of the Book of Number series, as well as a wide range of short stories and books of Modern Myth.

From the Threads of Fate Weave the Garment of your Destiny

www.ingramcontent.com/pod-product-compliance
Lightning Source LLC
Chambersburg PA
CBHW030657230426
43665CB00011B/1130